Fitting supervision to offenders: assessment and allocation decisions in the Probation Service

by
Ros Burnett

*Research Fellow and Head of
the Probation Studies Unit*
Centre for Criminological Research
University of Oxford

A Research and Statistics Directorate Report

Home Office
Research and
Statistics
Directorate

London: Home Office

Home office research studies

The Home Office Research Studies are reports on research undertaken by or on behalf of the Home Office. They cover the range of subjects for which the Home Secretary has responsibility. Titles in the series are listed at the back of this report (copies are available from the address on the back cover). Other publications produced by the Research and Statistics Directorate include Research Findings, the Research Bulletin, Statistical Bulletins and Statistical Paper.

The Research and Statistics Directorate

The Directorate consists of three Units which deal with research and statistics on Crime and Criminal Justice, Offenders and Corrections, Immigration and General matters; the Programme Development Unit; the Economics Unit; and the Operational Research Unit.

The Research and Statistics Directorate is an integral part of the Home Office, serving the Ministers and the department itself, its services, Parliament and the public through research, development and statistics. Information and knowledge from these sources informs policy development and the management of programmes; their dissemination improves wider public understanding of matters of Home Office concern.

First published 1996

Application for reproduction should be made to the Information Section, Home Office, Room 278, 50 Queen Anne's Gate, London SW1H 9AT.

©Crown copyright 1996 ISBN 1 85893 599 7
ISSN 0072 6435

Foreword

A key finding to emerge from research on 'what works' in reducing offending is the importance of tailoring intervention to individual offenders. Systematic assessment is also vital if public and sentencer confidence in the probation service is to be maintained. This study was commissioned to discover how senior probation officers allocate offenders to particular supervisors, and how probation officers then assess those they are supervising. It identifies a wide range of techniques and highlights those which offered most scope for ensuring that offenders are allocated and assessed in ways which reduce risk and increase the chance of reform.

CHRIS LEWIS
Head of Offenders & Corrections Unit,
Research & Statistics Directorate

Acknowledgements

This research was commissioned by the then Home Office Research and Planning Unit (now reorganised into the Research and Statistics Directorate). I am grateful to the following for helping me identify key issues to address in the research interviews: Colin Roberts, Department of Applied Social Studies, University of Oxford; David Faulkner, St John's College, Oxford; and George Mair, (then) Principal Researcher at RPU. I thank Carol Hedderman, Research and Statistics Directorate, for helpful comments on various drafts of the report, along with Ed Mortimer and members of the Probation Service Division and HM Inspectorate of Probation. Roger Hood, Director of the Centre for Criminological Research, and Andrew Sanders, Deputy Director, provided vital support and advice.

The following probation services were included in the study: Berkshire, Dorset, East Sussex, Gloucestershire, Greater Manchester, Kent, Leicestershire, Northumbria, Hereford and Worcester, and South Yorkshire (preceded by some pilot interviewing in Northamptonshire, Oxfordshire and Warwickshire). I am greatly indebted to all of the practitioners and middle managers who talked to me about the tasks and challenges of community supervision.

I would particularly like to thank Hannah Bichard for transcribing endless hours of interview tapes; others who assisted were Martha Kempton and Humaira Ahmed. Anja Spindler facilitated the statistical analysis, and Heather Hamill helped with the data entry and coding.

ROS BURNETT

Contents

Summary

Background

One of the key findings to emerge from research on 'what works' in reducing offending is the importance of matching the various forms of intervention to individual offenders. This study, commissioned by the Home Office Research and Statistics Directorate, examined aspects of probation practice which can affect offenders' chances of being allocated to various programmes and service provisions. It examined: the systems and criteria senior probation officers (SPOs) employ when they assign probation officers (POs) to prepare pre-sentence reports and to supervise offenders; their views on the goals of community supervision; the content of supervision; and the extent to which officers value and make use of special programmes in supervising an offender.

To this end, interviews were carried out with a total of 80 probation officers and 40 senior probation officers drawn from four teams in each of 10 probation services. Documentation such as corporate plans and statistics were also examined in all 10 areas, and discussions with senior managers were also held in some areas.

Systems and criteria for assigning cases

A number of different systems for assigning pre-sentence report (PSR) preparation and supervision were operating in the 40 teams included in the study. For example, in some teams allocation meetings were held in which probation officers were consulted by their SPO and could bid for a particular case; in others, cases were assigned on the basis of a rota or according to workload. The extent to which SPOs took an active part in assigning reports and cases also varied: one SPO had delegated responsibility to a clerical officer, another rotated the task between different team members.

It was generally acknowledged that allocation meetings could be time-consuming and a cause of delay, although probation officers welcomed the chance to have their preferences and interests taken into account. On the other hand, one innovative system, in which PSR appointments were allocated to set times for each officer, was very popular because it meant that offenders left court with arrangements made, and therefore resulted in fewer broken appointments.

Sometimes one factor – such as the area in which the defendant resided – was consistently treated as more important than other factors but, more often, a number of factors were taken into account. These included the size and equity of officers' workloads (virtually always an issue), avoiding delays, an officer's previous experience of an offender or type of offender (for example, when the case concerned sex offending or involved a female offender).

In all but five of the 40 teams visited, PSRs were prepared by the officer who was likely to become the offender's supervisor. This arrangement was generally preferred because the run-up to appearing in court and being sentenced was considered to be an especially opportune time for gaining insight into the offender's problems, and the point at which an offender was most highly motivated to take part in forming a plan to change. Indeed, four in ten respondents said the PSR stage was critical for offender engagement with the supervisor. However, many of the same officers also said that the constraints and pressures on defendants at that time may also mean that they (wilfully or unconsciously) present a false or limited picture of their problems. Interviewees supported this by citing a number of examples of unsatisfactory assessment and planning at the PSR stage. Moreover, in one area, where PSR writing and responsibility for supervision had been separated, the SPOs – and some POs – disputed that PSR writers who become supervisors begin with a head-start.

The goals of supervision

The principal goal for officers when supervising an offender in the community is the reduction of reoffending. Those interviewed were close to unanimous about this (93%) – though a number mentioned one or more additional goals – in particular: protection of the public (17%); rehabilitation and change in general (15%); and assisting with welfare needs (23% POs; 10% SPOs).

Well over half (62%) felt that their view of the goals of supervision was the same as the official goals of the probation service. The others experienced some tension between their own view and their view of official expectations, which they saw as too exclusively focused on restriction of liberty (52%) and on reducing offending behaviour (31%) to the exclusion of the social work and welfare-related aspects of the work.

The content of supervision

In all 10 of the areas studied, individual or one-to-one work with offenders was at the core of supervision programmes. Typical practice consisted of working, in a task-centred way, from a supervision plan, which was drafted and negotiated with the offender at the PSR stage and reviewed on a quarterly basis.

Half of the practitioners interviewed did not identify themselves with any one approach to the exclusion of others, but described themselves as drawing on a variety of theories and approaches. Two-thirds of the seniors endorsed this view of officers as essentially "eclectic" in their use of methods and of theories. But close to a third of the seniors said officers were increasingly adopting a cognitive-behavioural approach, and close to a third of the practitioners did indeed identify with this.

Three-quarters of the SPOs and two-thirds of the POs said that probation officers worked more or less autonomously: despite the increase in monitoring of their work and the extra rigours imposed by National Standards, the day-to-day decisions affecting supervision, use of resources, and the nature of the one-to-one work undertaken, were largely a matter for the supervising officer.

Assessments and referrals

Areas varied in their assessment policies for groupwork requirements: in some, group-workers made the assessment, but in others the decision about suitability was left to the report writer or supervisor. Assessment activities were mostly concentrated at the PSR stage (not surprisingly, given that this is a purpose of the report).

Most teams had some form of PSR 'gate-keeping' or quality control procedure whereby colleagues were consulted about the content of reports. However, once an order had been imposed, there was little by way of *formal* input from colleagues and other agencies in most teams, aside from the time left for this in formal meetings with seniors. A quarter of the SPOs were of the opinion that – because of other demands on their time – they were not doing enough to assist officers in their team with the task of carrying through supervision. Although a quarter of the 40 teams visited had a slot for case discussion in their general team meetings, there were only two where meetings were held specifically for the purpose of case discussion.

Assessment procedures were more clearly regulated in certain types of cases. For example, PSRs on sex offenders were based on more interviews than was typical, and sometimes co-workers were assigned to prepare the PSRs and to supervise sex offenders. There were also regulations about the checks, which should be made where child protection might be an issue, and there were instances of assessment meetings and additional oversight by management in respect of offenders identified as 'high risk'.

Although referrals to groups, specialists and community resources were not infrequent, there was considerable variation in how much the supervision concentrated on the one-to-one work if such referrals were not actually written into the court order. Some officers were much more active than others in making such referrals and in facilitating offenders' use of resources. Altogether, about six in ten of the POs were confident that they made sufficient use of the resources available to support their supervision practice. SPOs were somewhat less sanguine.

The most frequently mentioned reasons for not proposing referrals to group programmes were: doubts about whether the offender could realistically be expected to keep up with the attendance requirement; and uncertainties about the suitability of the group programme for the offender – for example, if the content was seen as too broad to be relevant; or if the content was seen as too educational and impersonal. There was a tendency to 'play safe' by concentrating on one-to-one work in case a group referral turned out to be counter-productive.

Referrals were more likely to be made if the group programme or specialist resource matched an individual's pattern of offending, or when it had a good reputation. A critical factor was, quite simply, whether officers knew enough about the resource to make a judgement about its potential usefulness. Therefore, publicity, good liaison and feedback, and experience of co-leading the programme were all important.

Local circumstances and policies also affected the use of groups and programmes. For example, setting targets for the use of particular facilities; and arranging for serious offenders to be automatically assessed for group programmes are both likely to increase referral rates.

Conclusions

These findings primarily reflect the views of probation officers who actively assess and supervise offenders and their immediate managers – SPOs. While it is clear that this focus was both appropriate and necessary, the perspectives of senior probation managers, sentencers, and offenders should also be taken into account. That said, the information gathered in this study suggests that while some areas have developed good systems for assessing offenders and matching offenders to supervisors, in others it is much more hit or miss.

Regardless of how skilled, competent or well-trained, individual practitioners are, in some teams they are left to shoulder too much of the responsibility for the on-going assessment and supervision of offenders. Scheduled case discussion meetings would help guard against discriminatory supervision, and facilitate the sharing of skills and knowledge. More opportunities for co-working might also be beneficial.

The systematic assessment of offending-related needs is central to ensuring the accuracy of probation assessments, and the confidence sentencers have in them. One way of achieving this would be to ensure that every offender passed through an assessment programme before and/or after sentence. Other measures for making the assessment process more systematic (which might also form part of an assessment programme) include the use of validated assessment tests; the formulation of explicit referral policies for each programme and partnership arrangement; the use of printed assessment guides and frameworks; the creation of structured forms for supervision plans and quarterly review forms; and the compilation of resource directories and databases which should be made available to each team.

The question of voluntary attendance versus required attendance on group programmes needs to be examined to discover: relative referral and attendance and completion rates; and the effects of attendance rules on programme integrity and outcome (including breach).

Finally, in considering appropriate court disposals, probation officers and sentencers need to be well-informed about research findings on 'what works' so that offenders can be appropriately targeted.

1 Allocating offenders to community supervision programmes

Targeting: 'Horses for Courses'?

Research efforts have intensified to isolate the factors which most contribute to positive results when working with offenders. One of the key findings to emerge from such research is the importance of matching the various forms of intervention to individual offenders, taking account of such factors as their criminogenic needs (problems associated with offending, such as alcoholism or debt), 'responsivity' (or learning styles) and risk classification. (For factors in "what works" see, for example, Lipsey and Wilson, 1993; McGuire, 1995.) At the same time, there have been developments[1] within the criminal justice system generally, and in the probation service in particular, which have accumulated to move the supervision of offenders in the community closer to being uniform, systematic and purposely focused on the reduction of offending behaviour.

Nevertheless, there remains much scope for variation in supervision plans and programmes[2] provided for offenders in the community, as the following hypothetical comparison illustrates:

> Two offenders, both living in different counties, are each convicted of equivalent GBH offences. They have an equal number of previous convictions for violence and similar other offences, and both have an entrenched alcohol problem. Offender A is made subject to a 12-month probation order with a requirement to attend an anger management group, while offender B is sentenced to a two-year probation order with no requirements. During the course of their orders, B's probation officer provides one-to-one alcohol counselling, while A's probation officer refers him to the Community Alcohol Team for similar counselling.

There are numerous factors which individually or collectively might explain these variations in supervision, some attributable to area resources, some to

---

[1] Not least, several changes in criminal justice legislation since the beginning of the 1990s, the Audit Commission (1989) inquiry into the probation service, the introduction of 'managerialism' into the probation service (see for example, Statham and Whitehead, 1992), the introduction of national standards for the work of the probation service.

[2] The term 'programme' is used generically in this report, to refer to any plan of work for supervising offenders, whether on an individual basis (and including various referrals which may be made to other services) or in a group-work setting.

sentencers, some to offenders and others to probation officers. For instance, the alternative sentences may have arisen because of where the offenders reside (differences in partnership arrangements and group provision; local sentencing patterns). Perhaps the alternative approaches to the drink problem reflect practice preferences, one officer tending to make more than the other of statutory and voluntary agencies in the community. However, these differences may stem from the contrasting needs of these two particular offenders, concealed by their similar offending profiles: both the sentences and the subsequent decisions might therefore be testimony to careful pre-sentence and post-sentence assessments.

Whatever the explanation may be, the different courses of supervision for offender A and offender B are arguably discriminatory, and are of particular concern if it can be shown that elements of one programme are more likely than the other to be associated with reduced reoffending. Disquiet has been expressed in different quarters about the adequacy of procedures and practices by which offenders are targeted for probation service programmes that is, whether assessment is precise and rigorous enough (Roberts, 1993); whether assessment and choice of methods are subjective (MacDonald, 1993); whether the value-base of officers leads to indirect discrimination and to under-use of special projects (Grapes, 1994); and the disparity between services in their approaches to corresponding specialist projects (Mair, 1993).

A study in ten probation service areas

Aims

The purpose of the present project was to find out more about what aspects of probation practice can affect offenders' chances of being allocated to the various programmes and service provisions. An assumption was made that allocation decisions are largely linked to assessment decisions, and therefore, in this research, the two processes were treated as inter-related. The project was focused on the insights and experience of those with key responsibility for community supervision: probation officers (POs) whose work included supervision of probation orders, and senior probation officers (SPOs) with a management responsibility for the work of these officers. In addition, limited information was obtained from higher management, probation centre managers, information and research officers, and documentation from the service areas included. To keep the scope of the inquiry within manageable proportions, the important parts played by sentencers, and by the offenders themselves were not directly examined.

The specific aims were:

- to ascertain what criteria are applied by managers when they assign officers (a) to prepare pre-sentence reports, and (b) to supervise offenders after court orders have been imposed

- to explore officers' views of the goals, modes and methods of community supervision, the range of resources available and referrals which can be made, and their usage of those resources

- to explore what sources of information, offender assessment strategies, and allocation criteria, are used by probation officers when they recommend specific programmes for offenders on whom they prepare pre-sentence reports

- to explore what sources of information, assessment strategies and criteria are applied by supervising probation officers and their managers in following through pre-sentence report suggestions once responsibility for supervising an offender has been assigned

- to compare the assessment and allocation practices and intervention practices of various probation service areas in order to identify problems and strengths associated with different practices, and to make recommendations for improvements to practice.

Who was interviewed?

The information was obtained primarily by means of in-depth interviews with 80 probation officers (POs) and 40 senior probation officers (SPOs). Ten counties were included; in each county, four teams[3] were visited, and in each team two probation officers and one senior were interviewed. In some of the counties, discussions took place with higher managerial staff and with managers of groupwork programmes. Documentation (e.g. corporate plans, statistics, groupwork publicity) was examined for each county. The main investigation (i.e. of ten probation service areas) was preceded by preliminary investigation and piloting at three different probation service areas.

---

3   Teams have traditionally been generic in function (that is, each PO participates in all aspects of the service's work and has a mixed caseload), and distinguished from one another simply by location of the office building in which they work – though in larger conurbations more than one such team may be housed under the same roof, each with its own SPO. The majority of teams included in this study were of this generic type, albeit affected in varying degrees by a gradual trend towards syphoning off some aspects of the work to specialist officers (e.g. for sex offenders) and to specialist teams distinguished by function. The latter include teams responsible for court work; for through-care; and for civil and matrimonial work. All the teams in this study were involved solely or partly in community supervision, but, as is mentioned in Chapter 2, five of the teams were less involved in PSR preparation because this had been made, by and large, the responsibility of a specialist court team.

Selection of probation service areas

The ten probation service areas which were included in this project were Berkshire, Dorset, East Sussex, Gloucestershire, Greater Manchester, Kent, Leicestershire, Northumbria, Hereford and Worcester, and South Yorkshire. In addition, some piloting was undertaken at Northamptonshire, Oxfordshire and Warwickshire. To guard the confidentiality of those interviewed, these services are not distinguished by name in the body of this report.

The areas were chosen with a view to including a variety of metropolitan, shire and rural counties, on the assumption that administrative and practice considerations can differ depending on the location. The four teams within each county were chosen by senior managers of that area.

Form and content of interviewing

The interviewing employed a semi-structured format, allowing for exploration of differences in practice as well as covering the common ground. The issues covered in the interviews were as follows:[4]

- *overview of community supervision*: goals; modes of intervention; main way of working to reduce offending; main obstacles; views on the National Standards; views on increased monitoring of probation work; and of increased partnerships with other agencies; job satisfaction

- *one-to-one work and referrals*: methods, techniques and theories; home visits; use of volunteers; criteria for proposing groups when writing pre-sentence reports (PSR); post-sentence referrals; general reservations about referral

- *resources in the probation service area*: overview of what is available for use with probationers;[5] gaps and strengths; favoured resources and reasons for their use; less favoured resources and reasons for under-use; self-assessment of practitioners' overall knowledge and use of resources

- *assignment of work to officers*: how PSRs are allocated; how community orders are allocated; evaluation of the allocation system

---

4   The main questions asked are listed in the Appendix.
5   'Probationers' is used in this report to refer to those subject to probation orders, supervision orders and combination orders. Although the term 'client' continues to be used by many within the service – if only because it readily distinguishes offenders for whom the service has a supervisory responsibility – it is increasingly regarded as a label which is incongruous with the nature of contractual obligations between offenders and their supervisors (see for example, Bryant, 1991).

- *assessment of offenders*: when, what and how offenders are assessed; verification and consultation; systematic procedures and tools in use; monitoring of PSR assessment; consultation, assistance and monitoring for on-going assessment and supervision

- *consistency and effectiveness*: consistency in PSR proposals; consistency in supervision programmes; perceived factors in effective supervision.

Although the interviewees were primarily invited to generalise about assessment and allocation practice, in relation to the above questions, some randomly selected cases (three probationers for each of the 80 practitioners included in the study) were drawn on for further detail and in order to obtain specific examples of the general points being made.[6]

Outline of the report

Chapters 2 and 3 of what follows are concerned with the fundamentals on which assessment and allocation of offenders are based. Chapter 2 looks at the criteria for assignment of work to officers, including the preparation of pre-sentence reports, and the supervision of court orders. Chapter 3 is concerned with the officers' accounts of the goals, means and methods of community supervision programmes.

Chapter 4 looks at the various resources (groups, partnership schemes, community services) to which offenders might be referred. Section A is concerned with the views and attitudes of probation staff about using these various resources, and the general criteria which informs such referrals. Section B summarises views of the resources available in the probation service areas investigated, and analyses reasons given for good use of some resources and under-use of others.

The steps involved in the assessment process are turned to in Chapter 5: what is being assessed, how it is being done, and with what systems, procedures and consultations? Although there is some overlap, the pre-sentence assessment leading to the court report is addressed as a separate process from the assessment which continues after a person has been sentenced to supervision by the probation service. Officers' views on the perceived adequacy and consistency of assessment and programme matching are summarised. In the final Chapter, implications are drawn for the improvement of matching offenders to programmes.

---

6   A separate quantitative analysis of the case records and related interview data in respect of these 240 offenders is being undertaken. A separate report will be produced shortly as the issues addressed go beyond the scope and aims of the present study.

2 Assigning responsibility for assessment and allocation

Stages of assignment[1]

There are two distinct stages for assessment and allocation of offenders, both requiring separate decisions regarding who should be assigned the responsibility: (1) preparation of a pre-sentence report (PSR); (2) supervision, once an order has been imposed. Typically, the responsibility at each stage is assigned to a single member of staff (though sometimes two officers are assigned in the case of sex offenders). It was found that the criteria and the procedures for assignment of responsibility differ considerably, with the variation occurring more at team level than at county level.

Assignment of pre-sentence reports

One or more of the following factors might be taken into account when assigning PSRs: whether the defendant is already known to an officer; staff specialisms; the needs of students and first-year officers to gain experience of different types of offending; officer workload; where the defendant lives; the gender or ethnicity of the defendant. However, approximately half of the staff interviewed thought that a workload or quota basis was the main criterion (see Table 2.1). Assignment by matching of offence type to officers' specialisms or practice needs was rarely identified by staff as the *most* important consideration, yet such matching was mentioned as one of the deciding issues by nearly half of POs and three-quarters of SPOs (see Table 2.2). Around a third of the interviewed (30% of POs and 40% of SPOs) included officers' self-selection to prepare the report as one factor, that is, officers volunteering or declining to take on PSRs.

---

1   The term 'allocation' is mostly used within the probation service to denote allocation of work (as in 'allocation meeting', 'numbers of reports allocated'). It also denotes, however, the allocation of offenders to resources (to specialists; partnership services; groups); in other words – to change the emphasis – the allocation of limited 'places' to offenders. To avoid confusion in this report, the term 'assignment' is used to refer to the distribution of work to officers, while 'allocation' is used more broadly to embrace all that an offender might 'get' during a period of supervision.

Table 2.1[2]
**Factors thought to influence assignment of PSRs
and responsibility for supervision**

	PSR assignment		Supervision assignment	
	Relevant factor %	Main factor %	Relevant factor %	Main factor %
Workload/quota	79.8	47.5	47.1	14.4
Geography	18.5	11.9	16.8	9.3
Officer (specialism/need)	55.5	2.5	44.5	2.5
Already know offender	28.6	1.7	5.9	0.8
Gender/ethnicity	16.8	0.0	15.1	0.0
Volunteering	33.6	4.2	52.9	4.2
Wrote PSR	–	–	83.2	48.3
Balance of factors	5.0	16.9	0.8	13.6
Not known (applies only to POs)	9.2	13.6	5.0	8.5

Table 2.2
**Comparison of SPO and PO views of main factor
influencing PSR and supervision assignment**

	PSR assignment		Supervision assignment	
	PO %	SPO %	PO %	SPO %
Workload/quota	43.0	56.4	11.5	20.0
Geography	12.7	10.3	7.7	12.5
Officer (specialism/need)	1.3	5.1	1.3	5.0
Already know offender	0.0	5.1	0.0	2.5
Gender/ethnicity	0.0	0.0	0.0	0.0
Volunteering	3.8	5.1	3.8	5.0
Wrote PSR	–	–	52.6	40.0
Balance of factors	19.0	12.8	12.8	15.0
Not known	20.0	0.0	12.8	0.0

2   All tables are based on the responses of 80 POs and 40 SPOs unless otherwise stated.

One in five of the POs was unsure about, or thought there was no main criterion for assignment. The following extracts exemplify the extent to which PSR assignment can be a balancing act for the SPOs involved:

We are trying to balance two or three different principles... We are trying to allocate on the basis of what staff and student needs are - in particular, for unaccredited staff... and then we are trying to allocate on a geographical basis to keep costs down, and we are trying to add on to this, who has got what specialisms. But I think that at the end of the line, we end up allocating mainly on the basis of who is actually available, who is going on leave, who has got the highest or lowest caseload. [SPO]

Really one ought to be looking for the best person to do the job, but the system doesn't work that way... Now the way I allocate reports at the moment is, there are in my head certain priorities. We have two first-year officers who need to have a range of work for their portfolios to satisfy. So, anything that comes in, if it looks remotely unusual or different, they get first bite. So, everything is initially scrutinised for value for the first-year officers. The next priority is the students. We have a lot of students in here at the moment and they equally have to build up a certain amount of work, so they get second choice. If there are no takers there, it gets allocated out. It then depends on, by and large, what the workloads are. There are a couple of people here who carry additional specialist responsibilities, so they will attract, like, sex offenders, or whatever. But mainly it depends on who has got the capacity to do it. [SPO]

The limited time available to prepare the report is an issue at the PSR stage. The interviews for this project took place when the revised National Standards were on the horizon.[3] One team (where less than half of defendants, in recent months, had kept their first PSR appointments) had introduced a system of pre-scheduled PSR appointments. The POs in the team provided times when they would be available for this purpose in the coming weeks so that, following adjournments for PSRs, the Court Duty Officer was thus able to organise an appointment and provide the officer's name before the defendant left the court.

In respect of five of the 40 teams included in the study, preparation of court reports was the specialist responsibility of another team: if the defendant was not already being supervised, it was undertaken by officers who did not have responsibility for supervision once orders had been imposed.[4] In the

---

[3] The 1995 National Standards require that pre-sentence reports are prepared for Crown Courts in advance of trial if possible, and "as expeditiously as possible" if an adjournment is necessary, and on the same day if the adjournment would involve a custodial remand (Home Office, 1995, Chapter 2, para. 46); and, for Magistrates court, to be prepared within 15 working days (ibid, para. 50).
[4] Services which split the responsibilities of court work, community supervision, though-care, etc. refer to their teams as 'specialist' or 'functionalist', as distinct from 'generic' teams.

teams visited where this applied, the POs wrote reports primarily or solely on their current probationers: in some instances, they also wrote a proportion of reports on unknown defendants when there was an 'overflow' of reports from the court team.

Assignment of responsibility for supervision

In the 35 teams where the tasks of PSR preparation and supervision were not separated, the most prevalent practice was for orders to be assigned to the officer who had written the report: thus, the choice of PSR assignment pre-empted the decision about who should supervise. ("By and large, where an officer writes a report in this team, they supervise".) But there were frequent exceptions to this rule of thumb. As was the case with PSRs, there may be several unrelated objectives to be met, so that assignment of orders is equally a balancing act (see Table 2.1). In one service, which included extensive rural areas, more home visits were necessary because of remoteness from the office, and orders therefore tended to be allocated on a geographical basis. Attempting to match the officer to the offender was rarely given as the main consideration, but was mentioned as one of the relevant considerations by around a half of those interviewed:

> *For allocation of orders, again, first-year officers need work, students need work, and only then do I allocate out to other staff. Then it depends on who wrote the report and whether they have the capacity. Some people have key responsibilities so they will pick up most of that type of work; for instance, we have one officer [who] picks up most of the female clients. You do have to have a bit of negotiation around a team, but once again there are priorities, and then, by and large, it's down to who has got the space.*

> *To a certain extent we allocate on the basis of skills and interests, but not as much as we would like. I mean, I have a couple of officers who are excellent on community care applications, getting offenders into Drug Rehabilitation Units, seeing them through and getting results – sometimes with people who have never before succeeded in treatment. They will get them through it if anyone can. So if a case comes along that needs those sorts of skills, I will allocate to the officer concerned. And I have been known to take other work away from that officer to allow them to take the particular person on. But the bottom line is having space. If they haven't got the space, someone else has to do it.*

Matching by specialism, in so far as it did happen, was in terms of types of offenders, or types of problems, rather than matching according to differences in officers' working style or differences in offenders' responsivity or learning styles.[5] To the extent that officers self-select (put in bids at meetings; opt out from supervision after they have prepared a report on the grounds that there is a personality clash) they may be acting on a belief that a matching between officer and offender with regard to personality (or rapport) is relevant to the effectiveness of supervision (see Chapter 5).

Who decides?

Some SPOs, but by no means all, take control of PSR and case allocation. They may do this 'behind closed doors' (sometimes with another senior where more than one team is situated in the same building), or at allocation meetings in consultation with the team. Where there is a specialist court team, PSRs are allocated by the SPO of that team. Teams which have allocation meetings, hold them on a frequent basis – anything from everyday to once a week. This arrangement (in theory, at least) enables officers to state their preferences or reservations or, if the SPO relinquishes the reins, to make democratic choices. The SPO is not necessarily present at meetings; they may be chaired by probation officers on a rota basis or by the previous day's court duty officer. In one of the teams visited the PSRs were allocated by a clerical officer on a numbers and rota basis. In another team (as mentioned in the previous section) allocation was, in effect, done by the court duty officer using a pre-scheduled appointments diary.

Is there a model assignment system?

Two-thirds of the SPOs were reasonably satisfied with the work assignment system for their team; that is, they thought it worked well or that no other system would be better given the circumstances (e.g. allocation by geography in a rural area). Fewer POs were satisfied (42%). This is not surprising, given that the SPOs had often introduced the system or were in a position to change it. There was often an element of experimentation with different systems, interviewees referring to recent or imminent changes: the SPOs were likely to have imported schemes from other offices or to institute modifications of their own.

Evaluation of the systems depends, of course, on which of the various objectives was considered to be the most vital. Issues which were recurringly mentioned as of particular importance were: (a) equitable distribution of

---

5   According to the 'principle of responsivity' (as set out by Andrews, 1995, p.43): "The most effective style and modes of treatment service are those matched with the needs, circumstances and learning styles of high risk individuals... Interpersonally and cognitively immature clients in particular require structured service; interpersonally anxious clients in particular respond poorly to highly confrontational services; other specific considerations may also be applicable for some subtypes of offenders".

the work, (b) speed (how much time was invested in making assignment decisions, and the delay caused by such decisions), and (c) continuity between the PSR stage and the supervision stage (that is, whether the same officer should perform both tasks).

With regard to equity, from the PO's perspective this was not simply a matter of the quantity of reports and cases they were assigned; it was also about variety in their work, relevant experience and not being overloaded with the most troublesome probationers:

> *Sometimes one is going about this looking for a least worst thing. You can see there are four or five cases coming and you can see there are two or three you don't want to get involved with. Sometimes it's a hiding to nothing, somebody I know who has been on probation a few times and I just know it's going to be a grind. I like to start with fresh people.*
>
> *[This order] was allocated to me when we had allocation meetings. I was newish. Everyone knew the offender. It was a case of: "Here, you have this one."*

Considerable time was saved by the SPO in the team where a clerical officer allocated PSRs (using a quota record and court diary, and without any reference to the type of offence or officers' strengths). This system, which the SPO had inherited, however, was disliked by the POs, who felt uncomfortable being assigned work by a clerical officer because of the reversal of their own professional status in relation to her, and who saw assignment as a management task involving professional decisions (e.g. some PSRs require more time and should be double-weighted; certain PSRs should be offered to the officer with relevant expertise regardless of whose turn it is).

In contrast to the latter, even though similar problems are likely to apply (that is, mechanistic decisions without regard to offence type or officers' interests), the team with pre-scheduled PSR appointments had welcomed the new system. It had provided additional structure to their time: up to three appointments a week had been organised without them having to make any of the arrangements themselves, and it had the advantage of securing quick PSR appointments (which the defendants were more likely to keep). The system was overseen by the SPO who made appropriate reassignments if necessary. Because of the success of this system there were plans to introduce it to other teams in that county. This service was thus overcoming a difficulty which continued to be a problem elsewhere:

> *We will have to deal with PSRs in a more efficient way. At the moment it is an inefficient process – there is too great a delay in securing an appointment.*

Allocation meetings were approved of by some POs in so far as they facilitate, at least in theory, an opportunity for them to express their preferences and indicate in each instance their capacity to take on more work. But those with direct experience of allocation meetings tended to describe them as problematic, in practice, because of the amount of time they take up; because expressing interest and willingness may be rewarded with an unfair share of the work; and because those too busy to attend meetings may find the least desirable jobs waiting in their in-tray. For these reasons, some SPOs were openly uncomfortable with the task of allocating work at meetings; and, partly to relieve themselves of the burden, some had handed over the chairing of meetings to POs, or had abandoned meetings altogether.

Many of those interviewed expressed the view that supervision benefits from continuity between PSR writer and supervisor. It was argued that supervisors who have not prepared the report are disadvantaged: the officer has had to get to know the probationer 'from scratch'. And the opportunity to engage with the offender at the amenable PSR stage had taken place with the PSR writer, who had negotiated and drafted the supervision contract:

Reports are the springboard to everything.

There's a natural progression if you wrote the PSR. It makes it much easier.

The officers believe there is value in the individual relationship that is forged in crisis at the report stage, which cannot be quantified but which, like Zen and the art of motorcycle maintenance, none the less we know is there. It is a very strong culture here.

One's motivation with people one has written a report on is higher because one has set the targets and said "Supervision would be appropriate and some good can come of it". There is a greater commitment if one has done the report oneself.

I have previously worked in a team where I did the majority of the PSRs for the team, and any orders were then subsequently allocated, and I didn't feel that was a good way of working. That was changed because there was so much resentment built up as a result of officers not being involved in PSR preparation. It can be petty, but there is a professional aspect to it, especially now that we need to be involved in contract-making at the PSR stage. The system we have here is better because it is about owning something. It is more motivating to write the PSR and then be responsible for the subsequent order. It is about owning it, and that is motivating. The probation service shouldn't underestimate the importance of motivation, especially in these times of cutbacks and cash restraints, which can be so demoralising.

From the offenders' point of view, it means that the officer they've met and with whom they've spent considerable time going into detail about their lives is the person they are going to be working with, and they are not going to have to go into that kind of information in the same depth when their order starts.

However, although some were strongly in favour of such report-to-order continuity (as the above extracts exemplify), when interviewees were asked about assessment at the PSR stage, such arguments were countered by claims that there is frequently a lack of openness and engagement at the PSR stage. That is, while there is little doubt that important groundwork and breakthroughs can be achieved at the PSR stage, it seems equally likely that a defendant may be reticent or misleading prior to sentence. (Further details, with examples, are given in Chapter 5: Assessment and allocation.)

There were other arguments both for and against a specialist system versus a generalist one. Specialist PSR writing was criticised as too like a "production line" or "sausage machine". Against the generalist approach, a few suggested that it is open to manipulation by officers to control their workload:

Human nature being what it is, some officers are going to be saying to themselves, 'Haven't I got enough cases? My caseload is going up'. And they are not going to propose probation – they are going to manage their caseload by not proposing it. And then in six months time I am going to do my survey and say 'Oi, you are not proposing probation; that's why your caseload is going down'. I can see the dangers in that and need to kick that around with my senior colleagues and my ACPO but also discuss it within the team as to how we want to deal with it.

One of the ten probation services included in this study had introduced specialist PSR writing in the mid-eighties. While it was generally agreed there were some losses, it was argued by SPOs that this specialist re-organisation had enabled a better service to courts, and that, in any case, initial objections had long since been resolved:

I know there was uproar when it happened because there was a lack of faith in colleagues' ability to assess, when you would then have to pick up whatever had been agreed with the client. But they had that debate almost ten years ago, and then I think they had three or four years when they still chuntered on about it. I think we have to have faith in our colleagues and to accept that their assess-

ment will be as good or as bad as our own... There are some disad-vantages - certainly from the perspective of the offender. The PSR and that level of interaction is a significant piece of work for the report writer and also for the defendant. We shouldn't deny that. They have engaged with it, and it can start a process... Unfortunately, probationers experience frequent change of officer for all sorts of reasons... For all sorts of arbitrary reasons, officers will change.

The PSR is seen as a piece of work that is complete in itself. It is an assessment. Offenders have not expressed a negative view about that. They are clearly told that if you get a probation order your probation officer won't be me... For supervising officers, what is important is that the PSR spells out why the person needs a period on probation, what kinds of intervention are likely to reduce this person's offending and what attempts have been made to agree with the offender a potential course of supervision. It has to be spelled out, otherwise there is a potential inefficiency in that officers who pick up the case can be going through the same process that the court officer went through... But I think the relationship between the two parts of the team is such that there is general agreement about what is an appropriate case for probation. Supervising officers work with what they get quite happily.

The other important issue, and the most frequently mentioned by those who felt there was room for improvement in their system, related to matching: whether the offender was getting the best officer for the job, or conversely, whether the officer was getting appropriate opportunities to use skills, to specialise, to gain experience, and to experience varied work. While it was recognised that officer-offender matching had to be weighed against other priorities, some felt that not enough emphasis was given to this and that the quality of assessment and supervision was therefore undermined. When interviewees mentioned officer-offender matching it was usually with regard to whether offenders with specific problems are being assigned to officers with matching specialist knowledge, or whether assignment of work is being matched to POs' learning needs:

We have quite a lot of specialisms within the team. I think these are a two-edged sword. We do have people in the team who have a special interest or special knowledge about mental health, accom-modation, drug and alcohol misuse and so on - and so in theory they can act as resources to other team members. It doesn't work very well because the people who carry these responsibilities see them as built-on extras and they are doing it with one arm behind their back rather than volunteering.

> *We have two officers who want to start working with a group of young offenders. So it makes some sense, if we get PSRs for young offenders, to give them those officers. And we have got an officer who wants to have a women's group in the New Year. So it might be appropriate to give her such cases. But what I fear is that they come to be regarded as The Drug Person, The Alcohol Person, The Sex Person, and they get all that type of offender and its gets very irksome. You do need a change and a blend.*

The issue of 'responsivity' and matching officers' approaches to learning styles[6] was scarcely referred to in discussions of assignment systems, the following reference being a rare exception:

> *It is good that officers have different styles and ways of working because often our clients are placed on probation more than once in their lifetime and they may respond to one person's style more than another's. That variety is a strength sometimes. It does cause problems in terms of matching officers to what that client might need and to what that particular officer can provide. That is quite random really.*

Among proposals for the future, one SPO was considering a move towards co-responsibilities and semi-specialism, with a view to two or three officers co-working with a particular type of problem (e.g. mental health) although their caseloads would not consist solely of people with such problems, and perhaps making use of other agencies and having a main reporting time when the co-workers could cover for each other. Similarly, another SPO (in another county) was encouraging officers to work in syndicates on a geographical basis. The plan was to have pairs of officers covering each side of the town, two taking cases from the west side and two taking cases from the east, with half the time of a probation service officer (PSO) allocated to each pair to undertake some of the more routine tasks. The intention was for the pairs to share their workload with each other and with their PSO, and to develop contacts with other agencies working in their geographical area, particularly police community beat officers, social services, and agencies involved in crime prevention.

---

6   The principle of 'responsivity' is defined in Footnote 5, in this chapter. Although given prominence in research on 'what works', as Lösel has pointed out, not enough is yet known about how differential offender characteristics affect the outcome of interventions (Lösel, 1993).

3 Supervising to reduce offending

Programmes of supervision

What the 'programmes' are

The label 'programme' is sometimes used narrowly to refer to meetings in a group setting, especially when there is a more formalised sequence of activities. In its broader meaning, programme refers to the sequence of planned work to be undertaken with an offender during the course of supervision. A programme may therefore consist of a variety of methods and techniques, whether used in individual counselling, or in any in-house groups or groups run in partnership, or in contact with specialists and other agencies. Such additional contacts might be requirements in the order, or subsequently organised and agreed with the offender. In this project, the concept is used broadly to incorporate the various types of work which result from assessment and allocation processes, including the work done on a one-to-one level.

One-to-one work is currently the basis for all that is undertaken while supervision is in force. Thus, even when there are referrals to groups, or to specialists and services in the community, these activities are usually woven into one-to-one work, rather than a substitute for it (although the one-to-one contact may be temporarily suspended, for example, while the offender is attending a full-time group programme). Therefore, referrals have to be understood in the context of one-to-one work, what officers are trying to achieve in it, and the assessments which are made in the one-to-one context.

Preferred modes of intervention

While viewing one-to-one work as central to community supervision, the majority of interviewees were in favour of groupwork and referral to other agencies or specialists for probationers deemed likely to benefit. In considering what should be the main way of working with offenders, there was an emphasis on selecting the most suitable method or methods on a case by case basis. Although few thought that a 'case-management'[1] approach should be the dominant method of working with offenders (see Table 3.1), there

---

1   'Case-management' is the technical term used in the probation service to describe that aspect of supervision concerned with referral (to groups, specialists, other agencies), and the management of such referrals. Case managing an order does not exclude working with the individual on a one-to-one level.

was, in principle an acceptance of it as one aspect of supervision; as one officer put it "I have very few cases where it is just me and the client involved".

Table 3.1
Views on the best way to work with offenders

	POs %	SPOs %
One-to-one	18.1	7.7
Groupwork	10.0	7.7
Case-management	3.8	7.7
Combination	10.0	23.1
Varies by case	53.8	53.3

SPOs were more likely than POs to stress the potential of a case-management approach; and those who were arguing for a combination of methods were often, in effect, promoting case-management:

> *The case manager approach is the right one, because there are things like employment, accommodation which are crucially important in terms of crime reduction which need to be addressed. I don't think that at the moment they are addressed fully by officers because they are still partly in the casework mode where people opt into these things if they think it is a good idea for their individual people, instead of having to do it as a system. The more you get into that the more you can see that the probation officer's style seems to get in the way. [SPO]*

> *Probation officers should only be involved in the offending bit. I've always believed in use of other community resources. It's good to formalise this...I actually now think that one-to-one is likely to be less effective. I would like to move away from the dependence on one-to-one relationships and the individual allocation of cases. A proportion of cases probably do need a close relationship with an individual but it can be volunteers who do that. Now that National Standards are more demanding we need to deliver the system differently... We need reorganisation of the way we work. [SPO]*

However, case-management is often seen in narrower terms, as a way of working which minimises or even precludes any one-to-one work:

Staff who have been around a long time are struggling to come to terms with the concept of 'case-manager'. [SPO]

Case management is the way that it is going. I have no choice but to go along that way because I do not have the time to work with people as I would wish. I am increasingly tending to refer... It doesn't give me 100% satisfaction because I am aware that the service I am offering to our clients is primarily to comply with National Standards and child protection issues, which have a priority, and making sure that the courts are serviced... What gets squeezed out is actually working with the clients. It feels not very satisfying at all. I find it quite difficult to be measured in my approach or very thoughtful about what I am actually doing. [PO]

What gets in the way is a range of feelings about "what is happening to my job, is it going out of the window? What does this case management mean? Is it an undervaluing of my skills?" There is a whole bunch of work that needs to be done at that level allowing them to explore what those feelings are and trying to challenge the negatives attached to that. Case management for example can be seen very negatively by officers, yet there are a lot of positives. These ideas come along and they are expected to be filtered from whoever has the idea say in the Home Office down through the various services, through chief officers, seniors and so on, arriving still attractive to people on the ground floor. That does not happen. What we need to do is to spend more time trying to sell these ideas to people. [SPO]

Only about one in ten POs thought that groupwork should be the main way of working with offenders (see Table 3.1). However, many identified groupwork as a particularly powerful way of working with some offenders. That is, groupwork was often singled out as the best mode of working with young offenders (because younger people tend to be more comfortable and responsive in a group setting), and with sex offenders (whose tendency to minimise and rationalise their offending is challenged when in the company of others).

Another mode of working which is being increasingly used with some offenders is co-working (two-to-one; or two-to-two if the offender's partner is involved). Co-working, used primarily for supervising sex offenders, was described by those officers who have experienced it as an approach which could be adopted more frequently with other kinds of difficult offenders or in particular situations (e.g. cases of domestic violence). As was mentioned in Chapter 2, some teams were planning work in this way more generally.

Goals of community supervision

The principal goal for officers when supervising an offender in the community is the reduction of reoffending. Those interviewed were close to unanimous about this (93% POs; 94% SPOs) – though a number mentioned one or more additional goals, in particular: protection of the public (17%); rehabilitation and change in general (15%); and assisting with welfare needs (23% POs; 10% SPOs). Very few (7%) suggested that keeping offenders out of prison was a goal.

More that half (62%) felt that their view of the goals of supervision was the same as the official goals of the probation service. The others experienced some tension between their own view of the purpose and their view of official expectations, which they saw as too exclusively focused on restriction of liberty (52%) and on reducing offending behaviour (31%) to the exclusion of the social work and welfare-related aspects of the work.

Supervision 'in a nutshell'

Asked to pinpoint the main means by which offending behaviour is tackled, the broad picture which emerged is that the work basically consists of analysing the offending behaviour (what led to it, what the underlying causes are, the context in which the offending took place). Insights are shared with the offender, leading to negotiations about various means of tackling offending-related problems, behaviours and thought patterns so that alternatives can be chosen.

This approach (sometimes specified as 'cognitive behavioural') was also mentioned with regard to work in a group setting. Also, referral for specialist help or groupwork was often alluded to as part and parcel of the essential way of working with offenders. However, the descriptions of 'how the work is done, in a nutshell', revealed a presumption in favour of individual work (or 'one-to-one work'). Other frequently mentioned aspects of working with offenders, were: crisis intervention at times of emergency (as when the electricity is about to be disconnected, or following a domestic dispute), and practical assistance (such as helping people fill in forms; providing information about financial entitlements).

One-to-one work

Techniques and theories

Asked which techniques and methods are frequently used in one-to-one work, most referred to some form of offence-focused work, and each of the following was identified by at least a quarter of both the POs and the SPOs:

- pen-and-paper exercises[2] (e.g. getting the offender to complete rating-scales on his risk-taking)

- graphic presentation (e.g. use of a flip chart sheet to illustrate recurring patterns of behaviour)

- motivational interviewing (getting people to the point where they are ready to face up to and work on their problems)

- counselling techniques (e.g. empathy; positive reinforcement; challenge)

- task-setting (i.e. specifying particular activities to be undertaken during the week)

- liaison, brokerage and referral (e.g. telephone call to Housing Department).

There were good indications, therefore, that probation practice has progressed from the traditional cornerstone of 'advise, assist and befriend' to more typically task-centred, behaviour-focused work. ("Officers are more authoritative than they were formerly"; "They have moved beyond the 'How's your father?' type of interview".) While discussion and a supportive manner remain basic ingredients, few (13%) suggested that this is how they largely spend time with their probationers.

However, there was variation in how specific practitioners were in explicating the way they work. Some were particularly vague about methods, and the theoretical underpinnings[3] of the work done with offenders – though sometimes defending this on the basis of a need to be pragmatic and theoretically eclectic.

---

2   Favourite sources for such exercises are: the Nottinghamshire Probation Service's manual *"Targets for Change"*, and McGuire and Priestley's (1985) *"Offending Behaviour"*.

3   The questions asked about methods and theories were open-ended, though in some cases, examples were given as prompts. Officers varied in how well-versed they seemed to be in the particular methods and theories which they labelled.

*I like to think I am using methods. I am pretty sure I am really.
I have been a probation officer for so long I have forgotten what
the labels are for different methods and theories.*

*I have always had a problem with hanging a label on the way
I actually work with individual clients… Basically, I am myself
with clients: what you see is what you get. I have always felt that
one of my main strengths is building up relationships very, very
quickly and putting people at ease. And I will let somebody know
what I think in no uncertain terms.*

*We talk about "challenging offending behaviour". But it is the
emperor's new clothes. Everyone labels it, but no-one knows what
it is.*

*It's a long time since I did my course so I certainly don't label what
I do. It would be behavioural, I suppose. Years ago I used a more
Freudian approach, looking at their early years and how that
affected them later – I don't disown that now; it has a part, but
I use it less. I try to deal with the here and now. My approach with
the offender is: "Because you are doing that and that, this is the
result. Do you want that result? If you don't, how can we go about
altering those results?" I find by and large, given the length of time
you do have face to face, that is the best use of my time and theirs.*

*One kind of thing that seems to be disappearing from the service is
this kind of theoretical discussion about what theory or method
you are applying with this person. [As a senior] I'm very rarely at
that level of discussion about people on supervision. It's quite often
"Have you identified the problem? What are you doing with those
issues. Has the person reoffended? What's the outcome?" That kind
of thing. Outcomes are now given much more weight over method.
In the past people employed a method and that was the end
in itself.*

Half of the practitioners interviewed did not identify themselves with any
one theoretical approach to the exclusion of others. Rather, they described
themselves as drawing on a variety of theories and approaches, though not
necessarily consciously, and open to using whatever is appropriate. Two-
thirds of the seniors endorsed this view of officers as essentially eclectic –
both in their use of methods and of theories. But close to a third of the
seniors said officers were increasingly adopting a cognitive-behavioural
approach, and a similar proportion of the practitioners (29%) did indeed
identify with this. The next most frequently mentioned theoretical approaches
were: psychodynamic (15% SPOs; 10% POs); task-centred (15% SPOs;

8% POs); brief-solution focused therapy (10% SPOs; 5% POs). A few practitioners (14%) said they adopted a non-directive, Rogerian approach.[4]

I try not to operate from any one single perspective. To do that is like holding up an acetate. All you see is what fits that perspective – and the other stuff doesn't. I try to keep myself open to things because otherwise it is too limiting. We should be more holistic.

It's a whole conglomeration of theoretical things that people are intuitively using. It's the end-product of a whole load of learning that's gone on, and it's difficult to pinpoint a conscious theoretical model.

Many SPOs distinguished between competent and less competent officers, often drawing a line between the more recently qualified and the longer-serving officers:

Officers are now better trained: they do a whole range of things, much of it quite focused on offending behaviour. They are less liable to be caught up in this endless problem-solving situation which I think a lot of us succumbed to a while back.

My impression is that people who are coming from training now come with quite a wide range of methods or techniques. That sur-prises me quite pleasantly because I don't think I was taught par-ticular methods when I did my training. Now as soon as they start in practice, officers will be using things like drink diaries or stuff from cognitive-behavioural programmes like Targets for Change, life maps, getting people to plot where they are on ladders and the cycle of change (the Prochaska and Di Clemente model).[5] So staff that are coming in have quite a lot of ideas at their disposal. The older officers are tending to stick with the one-to-one basis of "well, what have you been doing?" and "what shall we talk about today?"

Some staff have got what I call "a safe pair of hands". It is the less experienced officers who are the most competent...If you have got an experienced officer who hasn't got a question-mark, you are very fortunate indeed...When I came in the mid-eighties we had essentially a highly experienced staff group which meant we had a lot of deadwood, or people who didn't find change very easy. So it was very difficult to implement a culture change because people stuck their heels in. We now have a position of people much more amenable to change and with a lot of new ideas, and its very excit-ing when you talk to some of our new staff. They are coming off

---

4   Based on the "client-centred" approach of Carl Rogers (1961).
5   This refers to a model of change developed by Prochaska and Di Clemente (1982).

training, very enthusiastic, very keen, very bright… But what I equally see happening is people being absolutely worn out with the pressure that is around.

When the seniors were asked if they themselves adhered to or encouraged any particular approach, six in ten of the seniors indicated that they had no particular allegiance or that they favoured theoretical eclecticism. Just over a quarter (28%) advocated cognitive-behaviourism. Only two of the seniors associated themselves with a psychodynamic approach.

Making home visits to probationers

A fifth of the practitioners said they made regular use of home visits as part of supervision practice, while nearly a quarter said they rarely made home visits to their probationers beyond the minimum required of them. Reasons given for avoiding home visits were: the risk to themselves, the extra time required compared with office appointments, and the barriers against achieving the same quality of work, given the distractions of a home setting. Concerns about 'health and safety' have increasingly led to a policy of 'doubling up' for home visits, thereby adding to the planning and the time investment required. In the more rural areas, home visiting is seen as unavoidable: officers can be spending most of their time out in their patch, which may be very extensive. Others said they limited visiting to those people who are less free to get to the office for health reasons or because they are taking care of young children.

Most seniors indicated that there is variation between officers in the frequency and extent of home visits they make. Quite a few pointed out that newer officers tend to make far fewer home visits, question the value of them, and are more conscious of health and safety issues; whereas longer serving officers, who have been accustomed to regular home visits as a routine part of supervision practice, tend to carry out home visits more frequently.

The main benefit mentioned (by all those interviewed) was that home visits provide an opportunity to learn more about offenders in their domestic environment and in relation to others. Asked how home visits can be useful, a fifth mentioned that they are essential where there are child protection issues. Others (15%) found home visits useful in helping to build and reinforce the relationship with probationers, and a few (7%) referred to a practice of home visiting as the step before taking out breach proceedings for lack of contact. Seniors saw the general decline in home visiting as a matter for regret: only two suggested that home visits are of limited value, though many were sensitive to the difficulties entailed.

The autonomous supervisor

Choosing how to supervise

Considerable responsibility for determining what offenders get when they are subject to probation orders rests with probation officers (first, through the proposals and supervision plans in reports to court, and second, through decisions and steps taken during the course of an order).

While the frequency and timing of contact is prescribed to some extent by National Standards, nevertheless, three-quarters of the SPOs and two-thirds of the POs said that probation officers are largely autonomous in their supervising role:

> *One of the things that has struck me is how many people hold onto a notion of an almost independent practitioner. There is a resistance to the Service having a right to actually look into what they are doing and saying 'This is not acceptable' or 'This is the minimum we will accept'. I have talked about this in the team and with other seniors. It always surprises me when people take up that position.*

The rest (apart from one PO) suggested that the autonomy which probation officers have traditionally enjoyed in their supervision of offenders had, so far, only been slightly diminished by National Standards, increased monitoring and appraisal. Staff said they were still free to decide which methods and techniques to use in supervision, whether to refer probationers (with their agreement) to specialists and other services, how often to home visit, and whether to use volunteers.

The effects of the National Standards

At the time of talking to the interviewees, the original National Standards (Home Office, 1992) were still in force, but the introduction of the revised standards was imminent (Home Office, 1995).[6] Most regarded favourably, at least in principle, the establishment of standards in order for the purposes of consistency, accountability and providing guidelines. There was also wide agreement that the 1992 National Standards had been beneficial in practice: ("Left to their own devices, some POs wouldn't see people for weeks on end, while others would see them several times a day"). However, the majority (70% of POs and 84% of SPOs) regarded some aspect of National Standards as disadvantageous or problematic. The most frequently mentioned disadvantages of having to work to standards were: the amount of

---

6   The aims of the revised National Standards are to strengthen the supervision of offenders by setting out the requirements for supervision, providing a framework for accountability and by establishing priorities (protection of the public, effects on victims, provision of punishment) (Home Office, 1995, chapter 1, para. 5).

associated time and administration getting in the way of the "real work"; and an emphasis on the quantity of contact rather than the quality of the work that is done:

> *What concerns me is the way standards concentrate on things that are very peripheral, like amount of contacts... It almost allows officers to keep things at a very superficial level.*

> *[Supervision] is not just a question of getting someone to turn up for an hour once a week. The demands that we are making on that individual are more far-reaching. Therein lies the conflict and the nub of the problem for practitioners. The thrust towards a more automated way of dealing with offenders is actually seen as being incongruous to the role and purpose.*

Many were anticipating that the revised National Standards[7] were going to be difficult to apply or potentially destructive of the work being achieved because of the increasing stringency of breach regulations: officers argued that allowance should be made for the chaotic, disordered lifestyles of many people being supervised by the probation service. While many officers said they now valued the benefits of the first set of National Standards, having been uneasy about them when they were originally introduced, there was concern that the revised National Standards were out of touch with the realities of the work, and might undo the beneficial effects of the original standards. That is, it was argued that the increase in stipulated contact was too demanding, and it was anticipated (wrongly) that they would be required to institute breach proceedings after two missed appointments.

Monitoring of probation work

There were mixed views about the increase in the monitoring of probation officers' work, the majority of POs making both positive and negative comments (see Table 3.2). As with National Standards, some saw benefits in principle but were unsure whether they had materialised or felt that gains were outweighed by the increasing time spent on paperwork. Monitoring practices which were mentioned included various checks made on their work by others (such as checks by SPOs that National Standards are followed; 'gate-keeping' of their PSRs by colleagues) and the procedures they themselves have to follow to facilitate these (e.g. recording of PSR details and offender details; statistics on their use of resources; records of their use of resources). Around one in ten suggested that there was not enough information fed back to field teams, so that it was difficult to assess the usefulness of monitoring. There was a considerable amount of wariness

---

7   Drafts of the National Standards published in 1995 were being circulated at the time of these interviews.

about the ways in which statistics and monitoring may be used to 'manage' staff in the future. On the positive side, the potential for improving practice through appraisal and increased accountability was frequently noted. The SPOs made favourable comments about monitoring much more frequently than did the POs.

Table 3.2
Views on increased monitoring

(Multiple responses)	POs %	SPOs %
Positive comments	48.1	76.9
Critical comments	50.6	46.2
Wary/undecided	35.4	20.5
Not enough feedback	8.9	12.8

Job satisfaction for practitioners

More of the practitioners (50%) gained their job satisfaction from seeing positive change and improvements in their probationers than from anything else:

> *It is a feeling that you have made a difference – opened up an opportunity or brought about a change that otherwise might not have happened – anything, from a client having a different view on their relationship with their partner to a very tangible access to a benefit that they were entitled to but hadn't known about, or a better quality accommodation, or a grant to get some furniture. I don't think you can ever reduce it to probation officers coming to work to earn money. I think it is still about a core need of wanting to help people and making a difference.*

That such issues were emphasised in discussions of job satisfaction suggests that results of their work, irrespective of the mode of working with offenders, is of prime importance. However, the satisfaction gained simply from one-to-one work was mentioned by a fifth (21%), and four in ten (42%) spoke, more generally, of the satisfaction they derived from the opportunity to work with people.

4 Beyond individual casework

Deciding to use other resources

Awareness and extent of use

Three-quarters of the practitioners suggested that they were adequately informed about resources in the area or, at least, that they were one of a team which is collectively well-informed. Over half of the seniors (61%) concurred with this. Most staff suggested they were supplied with plenty of information, though some said that information could be made more readily accessible (e.g. collated into directories). There were rare instances in which a probation assistant or probation service officer (PSO), in the role of resource officer, collected and distributed information. The quarter of the practitioners who felt under-informed about resources, or that their knowledge was too superficial, or that there were significant omissions, attributed this mostly to insufficient time to inquire and to read.

Altogether, about six in ten of the POs indicated some degree of confidence that they make sufficient use of the resources available to support their supervision practice, but a similar proportion of SPOs indicated that usage varies from officer to officer (see Table 4.1).

Table 4.1
Use of resources for people being supervised

Do you / the POs make full use of resources?	POs %	SPOs %
Yes	58.3	30.0
Not sure	20.8	2.5
No, probably not	15.3	5.0
No, definitely not	5.6	0.0
Varies with officer	–	62.5

Referral to groups

There were differences between services in the availability and administration of groupwork programmes, which were reflected to some extent in officers' referral criteria. As with other service aspects, groupwork programmes were sometimes in the process of being re-organised or had recently gone through a reorganisation. The language for referring to groupwork programmes varies from county to county (reflecting legislative changes): references were to 1A(3)s and 1A(2)s[1] in some counties, occasionally to 4As and 4Bs[2] in others, to 'The Day Centre' versus 'Intensive Probation Unit' groups in another; while in some counties, distinctions were made by use of building and location names.

Referral at the PSR stage

The interviewees were asked about the general criteria they used, when writing a PSR, for proposing some form of supervision[3] with a group attendance requirement. The most frequently mentioned were the, often related, issues of offence seriousness, criminal record and whether there is a risk of custody. This suggests that, in line with sentencing guidelines, officers view attendance requirements, first and foremost, as a greater restriction on liberty than a 'straight' probation order (without conditions or requirements).

An over-riding concern, many said, is to avoid "setting clients up to fail" by proposing group requirements that they would be unlikely to keep. An offender may be perceived as someone who would not cope in a group setting because of difficulties relating to others, or as someone who could not realistically be relied on to attend because of their "chaotic lifestyle", or addiction problems. If there was uncertainty about whether an offender would fulfil attendance requirements, but it was thought that they could benefit from a group which addressed their particular needs, then voluntary attendance would be considered – that is, on the 1A(2) programme if permitted, or an alternative voluntary group. This was the theory; however, many were uncertain about which, if any, of the in-house groups could be attended on a voluntary basis (no doubt, partly indicative of organisational inconsistencies and changes of attendance regulations). Some Probation Centres require the offender to sign a 'contract of attendance' when there is an order with a groupwork requirement. There were instances where such

---

1   These allude to Schedule 1A of the Criminal Justice Act 1991, which gives courts the power to impose additional requirements in probation orders. Schedule 1A(2) is concerned with Specified Activities (including instructions to attend a group programme and to participate in activities) and Schedule 1A(3) is concerned with requirements to attend at probation centre. Other Schedule 1A requirements are: 1A(1) Residence, 1A(4) Extension of (2) and (3) above for sex offenders beyond the normal maximum of 60 days, 1A(5) Mental Treatment, and 1A(6) Treatment for Drug or Alcohol Dependency.

2   4A and 4B allude to Day Centre attendance requirements prior to the Criminal Justice Act, 1991.

3   The various forms of supervision include Probation Orders, the probation element of Combination Orders, and Supervision Orders.

a contract was used instead of a court requirement, but the contract was in effect given more weight by being written into the supervision plan contained in the PSR.

The proximity or timing of the group was another factor weighed in the balance. While officers said they did not let distance stop them considering referral, they thought that a condition of attendance makes more demands on a remotely resident offender than it does for those living in closer proximity; that is, it makes such a condition inequitable. Even though transport was likely to be provided or organised for those living outside the city or town where the group was held, it was often said that offenders viewed the prospect of travelling to the city, where the Probation Centre is based, as "like going to the moon".

Later referral to a group

As at the pre-sentence stage, there was uncertainty about whether offenders could be referred to attend the in-house groups after an order had been imposed. Most officers revealed that they had not attempted to make such arrangements. Three officers thought that it was possible to apply to the court for group attendance conditions to be added on to an order, but they were not aware of any instance when this had been done.[4]

Working in partnership with other agencies

Hardly any of the interviewees (none of the SPOs) were wholly against the increase in partnership arrangements with other organisations, and nearly a third were uncritically in favour. However, the majority mentioned some disadvantages and problems, or concerns associated with partnerships:

Table 4.2
View of partnership schemes

	%
In favour	29.9
Good and bad aspects	62.4
Against	4.3
Not sure	3.4

4   In fact, the sentencing principles of the Criminal Justice Act 1991 constrain courts' powers to add conditions to an order in this way as it would affect the proportionality of the punishment.

The difficulties identified were on two levels. Firstly, the expansion of part-nerships was described as a potential threat to the quality of in-house provision (41% POs; 58% SPOs), resulting from redeployment of financial and time resources, and as a gradual 'squeezing out' of traditional work by the increasing emphasis on case-management and referral. Secondly, there were complaints about the practical realities which get in the way of partnership ideals being realised (28% POs; 22% SPOs), such as the qualifications and staffing changes in the partnership agency, differences in philosophy, and failures of communication.

> *My nightmare about partnerships is whether, if we get very good at referring people to them, we end up with some kind of take-over bid or we do ourselves out of a job.*

> *I haven't got my head round that yet. I think it's about me feeling that this is another way they are going to be able to hive us off to privatisation. There's a bit of me resisting it.*

> *The concern I have is the money that is being diverted out and whether in the long term that means we are going to lose proba-tion officers, and expect other people, who are not properly trained or qualified, to supervise offenders in the community.*

> *I am a little bit concerned that the partnership thing is being pushed forward on a political tide rather than on it being demonstrable that it is value for money or that it is providing better services. We are in almost a silly situation now, casting around to spend five per cent of our revenue budget on partnerships. There is a bit of dogma there that I find difficult to get alongside. The service should be in a position to say we have looked around, and we have found nothing suitable, so we will either pass or we will employ someone directly to provide the particular service in question. That degree of choice is what the government should be prepared to give a responsible agency.*

The most frequent argument in favour of partnership arrangements was that they widen opportunities for offenders by facilitating their use of communi-ty services. The added advantage, it was often pointed out, is that they enable officers to concentrate more fully on their specialist domain: that of offending behaviour. A number of longer-serving staff referred to a tradition in the service of attempting to deal single-handedly with any and all prob-lems which an offender might present; partnership links were welcomed as a form of acknowledgement that the service "cannot do everything". Further, there is the potential for longer term benefits for the supervisee because use of that alternative service can outlast any contact with the probation service. Thus, the positive perspective on official partnerships is that they comple-ment the efforts of the probation officer.

I like very much the model of the programme that operates in [place name] where we have a probation officer who has a report centre in what is a community drop-in place that is provided by the voluntary sector. We pay for the use of a room there and we have funded a specific project there in relation to unemployment. The big advantage is that clients who go there to see the probation officer have ready access to a whole range of other services which they wouldn't so readily access if the Probation Officer were not there.

It is about actually going out to find things in the community, and feeding that information to offenders, who we come in contact with maybe for a very short period, and getting them linked to the support services within their own community so that they don't have to offend to get assistance. So when their problems continue or recur they can link in to the necessary or more appropriate support services. So I see partnership as very positive. If it is people with a drug problem - in the past probation officers have tried to deal with it themselves. They haven't got up to date knowledge, ongoing expertise. Therefore to link up and work with an appropriate agency, as we do here, we provide the person with the best service.

Use of volunteers

Practitioners seemed fairly divided in their use of, and views about, volunteers. About a quarter of those interviewed referred to problems of availability: there were difficulties finding the right person for the job being considered, or the system of recruiting was being reorganised, or else very few or no volunteers were available in that area. One in ten of POs was against using volunteers, while two in ten had 'not got around to' planning and organising volunteer involvement. However, the remainder of POs - close to half (45%) - were using volunteers regularly or occasionally: a quarter of the seniors confirmed that volunteers were being used by the staff in their team, while a third said usage varied from officer to officer.

Seniors were more positive about the value of volunteers (87% SPOs compared to 55% POs) and of the different ways they can be of assistance: whether by undertaking a more general befriending role, or by carrying out particular practical tasks. A third of all the staff interviewed were equivocal about the value of volunteers, referring to 'bad experiences' when plans have gone awry, or time has been invested without worthwhile results. Often stressed, was the need to have specific, clearly identified tasks when using volunteers, and the importance of careful recruitment and training of volunteers. Services seem to be increasingly appointing volunteer co-ordinators.

The resources

Views of area provision

Very few of those interviewed claimed that their probation service was badly resourced in the county as a whole, whether with regard to in-house resources, or to resources in the community, though there were some who were less positive in giving an overview of the resources for their own team and locality (see Table 4.3).[5]

Table 4.3
Staff appraisal of resources in their probation service area

	in-house %	community %
Good	39.7	50.0
Good for this team	16.4	14.9
Okay/could be better	25.0	21.9
Poor for this team	12.9	7.0
Poor	6.0	1.8

A comparison of the view of resources on a county by county basis (as far as might be ascertained from asking only 12 staff in each county) indicated that some services are better off than others. Two of the county services were consistently described in highly positive terms for both in-house and community provision. In another county, the community resources were estimated very highly whereas the in-house provision was viewed as relatively weak: this was a county in which community links with specialist access had been developed in place of in-house specialists. The views voiced in other counties were more varied, but in all of them, positive appraisals always outnumbered negative appraisals.

Not surprisingly though, there were some complaints from within teams which are remote from cities, and therefore disadvantaged by distance from resources: and there was some dissatisfaction in towns or cities which did not have a probation centre or groupwork programme. The more remote teams tended to have developed alternative arrangements (e.g. their own groups; link-ups with local resource centres; report centres in village halls for probationers living long distances from the office). Rather than concentrate efforts on using central county resources, some teams gave priority to

---

5   Community resources include partnership arrangements between the probation service and organisations in the voluntary sector.

developing local community links with a view to strengthening provision on the doorstep and so avoiding the extra time, expense and psychological barriers of requiring offenders to travel into unfamiliar territory; this includes examples in the suburbs of metropolitan areas, as well as in rural locations:

> *There are various valuable services within the town so we have networked with them... it means we can offer people choices of where to go for assistance. This used to be a very deprived area, very deprived. So a lot of voluntary agencies have sprung up to try and redress that void...We have decided to network so each officer would have responsibility for making contact with two of the agencies out there. From that, we were ahead of the partnership developments.*

Although 96 (80%) of the 120 staff mentioned at least one gap or inadequacy of provision, some of these were very specific, and none were referred to by more than a fifth of the whole sample. Most often mentioned were provision for mentally disordered offenders; provision for drug misuse problems; and provision of accommodation needs. More strengths in provision were mentioned than gaps (111 – 93% – of those interviewed mentioned one or more) but, as with gaps, there was no high consensus (as mentioned by more than a quarter of the sample). Between a fifth and quarter regarded provision for accommodation needs and provision for drug misuse problems as strengths in their area.

Possible deficits and strengths of provision appear to be area specific, though it should be stressed that no gap was mentioned by more than five of the twelve staff in each county. Table 4.4 shows all gaps and strengths in each county which were mentioned, in response to an open-ended question, by at least three members of staff in that county:

Table 4.4
Number of staff (out of 12 per area) mentioning perceived strengths and gaps in ten probation service areas

GAPS	A	B	C	D	E	F	G	H	I	J
Drug Abuse						5	3			3
Women								5		4
Young Offenders						3				
Mentally Disordered						3		3		
Accommodation			4	3					3	
Motoring Offenders				5						

Table 4.4 Continued

Number of staff (out of 12 per area) mentioning perceived strengths and gaps in ten probation service areas

Strengths	A	B	C	D	E	F	G	H	I	J
Drug Abuse			3	3	7					
Women				5				5		
Alcoholics			3		6					
Unemployed								3		
Sex Offenders			3				5		3	
Mentally Disordered			4				5			
Accommodation	3		3		3	4	6	4	4	
Debt Counselling								3	4	
Groups	9			7						
Specialists	4								4	
Partnerships				3	3	4		4	3	

These data need to be interpreted cautiously: gaps and strengths identified are likely to be relative to overall appraisal of the county service; they may reflect professional and personal biases and heightened awareness of the problems for certain groups. Also, the general labels belie the specificity intended in some cases (e.g. five in county D who mentioned a gap for motoring offenders were referring specifically to the absence of an in-house group for motoring offenders, excluding 'drunk-drivers' who are catered for; this gap was probably highlighted by the overall strength of the group programme in county D).

Some variations in resource provision

Specialists

All services had some in-house specialists. At the very least, they had probation officers described as trained to work with sex offenders.[6] Services also have officers who have come to be regarded as having special expertise (e.g. for work with young offenders; alcoholism) because of courses they have

---

6　They were not questioned about the form of training undertaken, but a recent survey of probation service sex offender programmes indicated that the type of training for this work can be anything from attendance on courses at the Gracewell Institute to an "unstructured apprenticeship" while helping to run sex offender groups (see Barker and Morgan, 1993).

attended and experience developed over the years; they may therefore carry a higher proportion of such cases in their caseload. Some teams have appointed probation service officers (PSOs) to liaise and provide information in specialist areas (e.g. accommodation; employment).

Services are also increasingly 'buying in' specialists as part of a partnership arrangement. The specialist (such as a community psychiatric nurse, a careers officer, or a Citizens Advice Bureau officer) may be based at a probation office on specified days. Even if such specialists are only available for any particular team on a fortnightly basis, being able to make an appointment for a supervisee to see them on that occasion is viewed as of great value, providing easy access for the person and freeing the officer to concentrate on other issues in one-to-one work.

Provision for women and ethnic minority offenders

There was more evidence of efforts to provide for women offenders than for ethnic minority offenders. The majority of the teams visited indicated that the latter issue rarely arises because of the infrequency with which the people they deal with are from an ethnic minority background. One of the metropolitan regions had organised a 'black empowerment group' but there had been difficulties getting sufficient numbers of participants. Many teams now ensure that females have the choice of a female officer to supervise them and often the same choice is extended for preparation of the PSR. A similar choice may be extended to ethnic minority offenders but, usually this is not feasible given the limited number of ethnic minority staff available.

The problem of group provision for women offenders was often mentioned. In areas which do not have separate groups for women offenders, it was said that women have occasionally been included in groups which are predominantly male in membership; but more often, the safer policy of excluding females has been adopted. In areas which have a women's group, there continues to be concern that there can never be the same range of choice in kinds of group provision for female as for male offenders. Further, a few expressed the view that women need to be provided with empowerment groups – regardless of whether there is a separate offending focused group for women – because their criminality is associated with their powerlessness in society.

Groupwork arrangements

A number of the groupwork programmes were in flux, or had recently changed: some were expanding their 1A(2) group programme and others cutting back; some were changing their 1A(3) programmes; some were

---

7   Footnote 1 on page 30 explains the terms "1A(2)" and "1A(3)".

changing venue or merging two separately located programmes.[7] Some probation centres had a rolling, modular programme, or there was provision for all probationers to see what was on offer and to be assessed for suitability. The groupwork programmes vary in length, in whether attendance can be on a voluntary basis, and whether entry can be arranged after a probation order has been imposed. Some 1A(3) programmes were described as including much physical and outdoor activity, while a number emphasised a cognitive-behavioural approach, along the lines of the programme first introduced by Robert Ross.[8] The fact that there was such variation in groupwork policies and management is perhaps indicative of the difficulty of 'getting it right'.

Well-used resources

The majority of those interviewed named one or more resources (group or partnership service) which, in their view, were of particular value for offenders subject to supervision by the probation service, or which were believed to be well used by colleagues. Of the 120 interviewees, 103 mentioned at least one group or service which they regarded highly or which was well-used.[9] Table 4.5 shows the most frequently mentioned reasons for favouring these resources.

Not surprisingly, the most commonly mentioned reason for favouring a group or service was that it was believed to meet a need: that is, it addressed a problem which applies to a high proportion of offenders (such as unemployment, and alcohol abuse) or it filled an obvious service gap (e.g. a group for women offenders). Nearly half of the POs favoured a resource because they had been impressed by what it covered (e.g. the variety of activities, the subject matter); some mentioned the specificity of content, rather than breadth, as a plus factor, an example being groups aimed at people with convictions for driving under the influence of alcohol.

> *I think the drink-drivers' group is excellent, and the net result for me has been that there's been an unusually high proportion of orders where I have been able to take them back for early discharge or early revocation – because the group has had such an impact... Parts of it are very powerful. For example, one week an ex-policeman comes along and talks about his daughter that was killed by a drink driver, and about the effect that has had on him and his family.*

Nearly half referred to the reputation and good results of a project (without necessarily knowing much about the content). Simply knowing what a

8   That is, the 'Reasoning and Rehabilitation programme', a cognitive skills training package, first tested in probation services in Ontario, Canada by Robert Ross and colleagues. (Ross *et al.*, 1988. See also Rayner and Vanstone, 1994; and Knott, 1995 for accounts of the version of this called STOP in Mid Glamorgan Probation Service.)

9   Altogether, interviewees mentioned groups or community resources 252 times. These included some which may be attended on a voluntary basis and some where referral is a requirement of a court order.

group programme is about or a service does (having attended or helped to run it at one time) was also given as a reason for referral.

Table 4.5
Reasons given for high use of groups and other resources

	POs N=69	SPOs N=34
(Multiple responses)	%	%
Meets frequent or neglected need	47.8	41.2
Impressive programme content	47.8	35.3
Good reputation/makes impact	47.8	29.4
Good liaison and feedback	30.4	17.6
Group leaders/well-managed	29.0	20.6
Community link-up	14.5	23.5
Know a lot about it	17.4	11.8
Proximity/accessibility	13.0	20.6
Positively viewed by offenders	14.5	8.8
Offence-specific content	13.0	8.8

Apart from the content of groups and services, how they are managed was also seen as important, as was the nature of contact between the resource and the supervising officer. POs in particular mentioned the value of good liaison between group leaders and the field officer, of 'hand-over' meetings when the offender completed the group programme, and of feedback information. How the groups or services were managed and run – the evident efficiency of the resource and the competence of key staff – were offered as a reason for making use of it by nearly three in ten of the POs.

> *The person in that post [secondment from another service] is enthusiastic, committed, really approachable, very positive in her work with clients and has her feet on the ground. She senses that it is no good talking about glitzy schemes and opportunities. You have got to be honest about where it is leading you and what will be at the end of it. She goes in with that very honest up-front approach in her work with probation officers. Their scepticism about 'Ah here we have someone who has just come to massage everyone into a scheme' disappeared on first meeting really.*

Two additional reasons, not so frequently mentioned, but nevertheless probably of importance were (1) that the group or programme was favoured by sentencers, and (2) that referral to groups saves officers' time.

Under-used resources

Some 1A(3) programmes have foundered from lack of sufficient referrals, leaving the probation service managers to ponder why. Was this attributable to, for instance, lack of information given to sentencers about when the programme is appropriately used, or lack of a clear enough policy about when to propose this as a condition, or mistrust at 'grassroots' level? Eighty-five staff gave examples of under-used resources, ranging from the full 1A(3) programme to specific groups. The reasons they gave are shown in Table 4.6:

Table 4.6
Reasons given for low use of groups and resources

	POs n=53	SPOs n=32
(Multiple responses)	%	%
Nothing specific	37.7	50.0
Unsatisfactory content	39.6	28.1
Accessibility	30.2	37.5
Management/leadership	26.4	34.4
Not enough attenders	28.3	31.3
Strict rules/breach risk	26.4	15.6

A variety of reasons were given for under-use of these resources. Four in ten of the probation officers pointed to some unsatisfactory aspect of content as one of the reasons. Either the programme was regarded as too packaged and impersonal, or too broad to be sufficiently relevant to an offender whose problems were more specific, or – the reverse – too narrowly focused, or there was a generalised impression that the programme was not very effective. Doubts about the content were mentioned particularly in the case of unsuccessful or struggling 1A(3) programmes,[10] which were criticised for being so broad that there was no readily identified content. Another related problem identified was that offence types and offenders may be too diverse to be easily addressed in a group setting:

---

10   Sometimes referred to as the 'full Probation Centre programme', and 'the 4B programme' (as it was named prior to the Criminal Justice Act, 1991). See Footnotes 1 and 2 in chapter 4.

For the Offending Behaviour Group, the offences can be diverse and the causal factors can be incredibly variable and yet somehow the criminal justice system appears to believe – and we stupidly go along with it – that you can put these people in a group and because they are all offenders, it will be okay. That's absolutely crass! I don't think we have done enough work on the offences themselves and the criminogenic needs.

Over a third of the officers, however, had not been able to point to anything specifically wrong with the content of under-used resources. Rather, they suggested that they (and colleagues) had not known enough about the resource, or that they had not deliberately avoided referral but the resource had not struck them as particularly relevant to offenders. There was a tendency to play safe by concentrating on one-to-one work: POs were committed to giving probationers the best chance to succeed in getting through their order, and needed to be convinced that attending a group would be helpful rather than counter-productive. As many as half of the seniors suggested that under-referral to particular groups was not specifically related to the content of a group. They suggested it was more likely to be a matter of oversight on the part of practitioners, or insufficient information about the resource, or a general wariness about making referrals unless there are clear, positive reasons:

There is some sort of mistrust at grass roots level and certainly middle management level of new ways of working in our projects team, and in a group work programme and that is not being taken up, or taken up in patches only. Some are not using it at all, others are. So the whole programme has a question mark over it. At management level it has been well resourced and a lot of energy put into it.

As was previously noted, officers needed to feel some confidence that an individual would be motivated to stay the course before proposing a requirement to attend a group; and another reason for low referral, given by a quarter of the POs, concerned strictness of attendance rules, and the prospect of breach proceedings for offenders who, though making some progress, find it sometimes beyond themselves reliably to keep appointments. Some officers believed that the rules about punctuality and acceptable reasons for non-attendance had been too strict, and argued that probation centre programmes should be run on more flexible lines:

One of the things that has struck me is that the criteria for entry into some of those group programmes are quite restrictive. One colleague had four clients he wanted to get involved in a violence programme and the team running it refused all of them. What is the use of a programme that has such rigid criteria that it can only take one small band of people who have a violence problem? Officers will say "That's not worth bothering about". It ceases to be a real prospect for officers to refer to.

The projects team are a bit elitist. I don't refer to [Project X]. What prevents me is that they have to be assessed by the projects' team workers. The chap can't get into the group unless they say yes. I don't want to have to go back to court and say "we have adjourned for this assessment, but the workers say he is unsuitable". That sets the guy up. The magistrates might think that if he is seen as unsuitable maybe he should go to prison.

As can be seen in Table 4.6 above, other frequently mentioned reasons for under-referral to groups by POs were: inaccessibility of the resource (especially distance from residential area covered by the team, but also the time when meetings were held, how frequently the course was run, and whether there were waiting lists); and dissatisfaction with how the resource was managed and led (disagreements with managers and group workers, a sense of exclusion, insufficient feedback information). There were some partnership arrangements which were criticised for poor liaison and unsatisfactory communication; a recurrent example was an agency working with substance misusers which had confidentiality rules which were perceived as a barrier to working in partnership.

Around three in ten officers referred to a resource failing to flourish for want of sufficient people to attend. This was mostly attributed to lack of interest or motivation on the part of the offenders. Examples here, paradoxically perhaps, include groups which in other areas had been described as omissions in provision: a women's group, a group for ethnic minority offenders, local voluntary groups intended as alternatives to a more centralised group programme.

5 Assessment and allocation

Assessments for pre-sentence reports

What is assessed?

The pre-sentence report assessment, according to most of the probation staff interviewed, is focused on analysis of the offence: the immediate context in which it occurred, the underlying problems and what might be a suitable disposal to propose to the court, taking into account the offender's attitude to the offence, criminal career and likely response to the different sentences which might be imposed. It was rare for anyone to mention assessment of the offender's personality, or of their childhood and background (about 5% in each case). Proportionally twice as many SPOs as POs (46% compared with 23%) stated that PSRs assessment should include the risk of harm to others. Only one PO and three SPOs mentioned that the impact of the offence on the victim should be included in the PSR assessment.[1]

A distinction should perhaps be made between assessment for the report and assessment more generally at this point in the process. As was often pointed out, assessment at the PSR stage is occurring at two levels: on one level it is concerned only with what is needed for the report, and on another it is concerned with offender assessment for the purposes of understanding the individual and his or her offending behaviour with a view to supervision:

> *I think that there are probably two different types of assessment going on. When officers are writing court reports they are assessing with a view to writing tactically in order to persuade a court that what we offer is realistic ... so I think the assessment is slightly angled in order to get the order we want, a kind of ends justifying the means ... But that has then got to be carried further between the offender and officer after the order has resulted.*

---

1   The revised National Standards stipulate that information on the impact of the offence on the victim is to be included in reports (Home Office, 1995, chapter 2, para. 15). They also give more emphasis, than the previous standards, to risk and protection of the public. Interviewing for this project took place before the revised standards came into force.

How the information is obtained

Apart from one or more interviews with the offender, the sources of information and consultation which were most often mentioned for PSR assessments were as follows (Table 5.1):

Table 5.1
Sources of information for the PSR

	POs %	SPOs %
CPS file	77.4	80.0
Other agencies	67.5	62.2
Probation and CS records	50.0	43.3
Other POs/SPOs	33.8	27.0
Group workers/CS staff	23.4	21.6
Offender's family/partner	15.6	16.2
Specialists (in-house)	11.7	18.9

The CPS disclosure file is perhaps the most valued source of information. If it is received early enough,[2] it enables the PSR writer to challenge the defendant's account of the offence should there be a conflict or omission of information – an important basis for open dialogue between offender and officer.

According to more than six in ten officers, there is likely to be some discussion with other professionals to whom the defendant is known (once consent to make contact has been given), such as the defendant's GP, solicitor, employer, or social workers in touch with the family. Checking seemed to be done more systematically if there was indication of mental health problems, or if there was concern about child protection issues. The extent to which other checks were made and agencies consulted seemed to vary from one to PSR to another according to the diligence, judgement or work pressures of the PSR writer.

There are in existence, various questionnaires, tests, and scales (not necessarily developed in the probation service) which can be helpful to aid assessment of offending related problems.[3] These have tended to be used mainly in

---

2   This was not always the case at the time of this study, but the problem of late receipt was more widespread in one county than in the others.

3   Roberts (1995) has advocated more use of such tests and schedules. Among examples he gives are: the Novaco Anger Scale; the Bangor Dyslexia Test; the Short Alcohol Dependence Data Questionnaire.

a groupwork context to assess suitability for attendance, and to provide group workers with before and after measures of an individual's problems and attitudes. But, with the exception of seriousness scales and sentencers' guidelines, and (less often) risk of reoffending scales, it was unusual for any tools to be used by PSR writers to aid offender assessments. Only six of the POs and two of the SPOs mentioned using anything of this nature for pre-sentence assessment. Practitioners often preferred to rely on their own experience, perceptiveness and ability to elicit disclosures from the defendant:

> *The tool I use is the gut... You can tell if someone is being cagey about something.*

> *It is more meaningful if you let the person tell the story rather than go through a long list of questions. If you ask a person questions in a disjointed fashion, you get disjointed responses out of context. Whereas if you get someone talking from memory, they are painting a picture and you find out more... Some people use lists, but to me that feels stultifying.*

In two of the counties, a framework to help structure and guide the PSR procedure was available, but there were mixed views on how helpful this was. In one case, criteria were provided in the form of flow charts to help in deciding whether the defendant might be suitable for one of the groups, and this was valued, especially by the newer officers:

> *The assessment framework provides a structure... There is a check-list of needs to help you refer to agencies and to groups, on the inside of the case management forms. This part is useful. It's good as a starting point.*

Referrals for assessment at the PSR stage

As was shown in Table 5.1, staff rarely said that they consulted in-house specialists at the pre-sentence stage (although, as has been mentioned, other agencies were likely to have been contacted for information in a proportion of the PSR assessments). Where offenders are seen by specialists in addition to the PSR writer, it seems that this is more likely to be as a result of formal referral procedures and court requirements, rather than at the discretion of the PSR writer. For instance, in counties where there is a diversion scheme for mentally disordered offenders, they are seen by a court-based community psychiatric nurse (appointed on a partnership arrangement), who, when mental health problems are suspected, is asked to see the defendant by the court duty officer, or by the police.

A key distinction is between referrals arising from case by case decisions, and referrals made automatically as a matter of policy, whereby every defendant, or every defendant in a certain category, is required to be assessed for a particular provision (e.g. as when all sex offenders must be referred for a sex offender group). Thus, the responsibility in these instances is not simply in the PSR writer's hands. The policy in some counties is for all defendants charged with offences over a prescribed seriousness level to be referred for 1A(3) assessment, that is, assessment for attendance on the probation centre's full programme. Similarly, there may be automatic referral for 1A(3)[4] assessment if the court indicates that an offence is 'so serious' that a custodial sentence is being considered. Sex offenders are automatically referred for psychiatric reports. Another system, halfway between automatic referral and discretionary referral, is when the PO is required to give a reason for not referring, once a group or advisor has been organised to meet a particular need.

There was often uncertainty about what referrals PSR writers are required to make for further assessment by others. Some mentioned the requirement to produce pre-sentence assessment for some of the 1A(2) groups:[5] groups for violent offenders were most often mentioned in this category. The nature of assessment for group suitability varies from a telephone discussion between PSR writer and group-worker, to an assessment attendance at the probation centre following which a suitability report is prepared for the court, to accompany the PSR. It may be that when defendants have an option about attending for assessment, practitioners take the line of least resistance:

> *Some officers are not referring people. Unless things are buttoned down well and truly, there are opportunities to avoid it... It's voluntary for clients. But there is no reason why officers shouldn't make a jolly good go at encouraging people to go...But I suspect a lot of the failures [to refer] are by default. People don't think. They are busy...*

One of the counties visited had set up an alternative system for assessment at the pre-sentence stage. Court officers were required to refer all unemployed defendants who had been adjourned for a PSR to the probation centre. At the centre, numerous assessments, and a file of information was then sent on to the PSR writer. As one of the practitioners put it "This means we are not going in blind" and, according to an SPO, it enabled the PSR writer "to concentrate more on what disposal the person needs and what will be done within that disposal, because some of the groundwork has been done; it is an in-depth assessment of aspects that we would never get time to do at the PSR stage otherwise". This scheme had been set up in partnership with NVQ Employment Unit, with a particular view to assessing employability (using

---

4   See Footnote 1 in chapter 4.
5   See Footnote 1 in chapter 4.

tests such as the Acid Profile Test), but with other assessments included. An additional purpose was to provide "a shop window", so that offenders could see what services are provided by the probation service. The system was criticised as in need of some refinement (for instance it was suggested that it led to some duplication in the case of someone being referred for the 1A(3) programme), but the main emphasis (from SPOs in particular) was on its benefits:

> *There will be all sorts of graphs and computer print-outs that the PSR writer will receive which the offender has taken part in at the probation centre. That frees up the PSR writer to concentrate on the offence and the reasons behind it and the best course of action to avoid reoffending: and this can be put into the sentence plan. [SPO]*

> *We certainly do a good job at the PSR stage. At the end of it, the PSR should clearly assess what we can do with that offender during the probation order. And, by then, the offender should clearly know what is expected of him or her. [SPO]*

PSR 'gate-keeping'

As well as obtaining help from colleagues on an informal basis, virtually all teams in the survey had a PSR 'gate-keeping procedure' (otherwise referred to as PSR monitoring or quality assurance). Various systems were in operation, ranging from simply asking any officer available to read through a report, to 'double gate-keeping' involving panels or a second reading by the SPO. A check-list was often employed in gate-keeping so that relevant issues were each considered systematically, and features seen as needing improvement could be more readily identified. In some teams there was a rota which gives all officers a turn in monitoring the reports of all other team members. Other systems described were: meetings to discuss problems before a report is written; partnering between two officers who then always check each other's reports; assigning the gate-keeping task to whoever is on office duty that day. To some extent, the system in operation reflected the size of the team. For instance, one officer in a remote rural post explained that there was often no other officer in the building to do any gate-keeping.

There were some criticisms of the system in use (such as the potential for biased choices in teams where report writers can ask whom they like to gate-keep for them), and a number of SPOs were sceptical about how well gate-keeping works in practice. However, almost all the POs were positive about the benefits of the procedure:

Table 5.2
Views on the usefulness of PSR gate-keeping

	POs	SPOs
PSR gate-keeping is:	%	%
Very helpful	55.9	20.7
Fairly/usually helpful	38.2	48.3

How critical is the PSR assessment?

The PSR assessment was described by many as vital for sentencing (27% of POs, 37% of SPOs), and as a critically important basis for the work which will ensue (38% of POs, 43% of SPOs). As was mentioned in Chapter 2, the PSR contact was held to have implications in several respects. At the time of facing an unknown sentence, offenders are likely to be particularly moti-vated to avoid further offending, and therefore responsive to suggested change and the steps which might be taken. They are also likely to be more communicative about their problems because of the stress of the pending court appearance and their recognition of the report writer's role. Officers included supervision plans in their PSRs – often presented in list form against bullet points – when proposing supervision.[6] Offenders were involved in negotiating the terms of the supervision plan and, in effect, entered into a 'contractual' arrangement. Four in ten of those interviewed emphasised the PSR preparation as the first stage of a working relationship and the point of time at which the offender is most ready to engage with the plan which is being set out. Very often the work has begun and some of the aims achieved by the time a probation order has been imposed.

Further assessment and allocation

Revision and change of the PSR assessment

When asked about assessment once an order for supervision has been imposed none of the interviewees suggested that assessment is complete at the PSR stage: 80 per cent specified that assessment is a continuous process, and many gave one or more reasons for further assessment or reassessment following the PSR (see Table 5.3). It was explained that the PSR plan is devel-oped and often amended during the initial stage of the order; some referred to the 'initial assessment' as occurring when the first quarterly review is written, even though the true initial assessment was, of course, made pre-sentence.

6   The revised National Standards include a requirement to include a draft supervision plan in the report (Home Office, 1995, section 2, para 31).

Table 5.3
Reasons given for further assessment or reassessment

	All %	POs %	SPOs %
Offender does not disclose all at PSR stage	34.5	36.5	30.6
Offender less motivated/relapses after sentence	17.3	12.2	27.8
Not enough time for assessment at the PSR stage	15.5	14.9	16.7
Another officer did the PSR assessment	14.5	14.9	13.9
Assessment is continuously refined	80.0	81.1	77.8

Paradoxically, in the context of why assessments are changed, lack of revelation by offenders was often the reason given for change of assessment, even though the PSR stage was said to be a point at which they often confess their difficulties and genuine feelings. Both situations may apply, of course, even in the case of the same individuals. As the table shows, SPOs more often than POs mentioned offender change of motivation and relapse once the order had commenced:

> *The information offenders are giving you is dressed up for court. We know that because the person tells you they are unemployed – so you perceive that as a factor in their offending. But after court, they quite happily tell you that no, no, they are always doing this painting and decorating. They don't want to go on some employment project. It keeps coming up this sort of thing. I had one recently: a young man with debts and fines. One of the reasons he offended was because of his debts. Afterwards when he was put on probation and I started talking to him he said "Oh don't worry about the debts" because the Provident money collector was his own mother. That does throw another light on his debts which one wasn't aware of before. When you make an assessment of somebody without the court hanging over it, you are airing the truth. You are actually in a position to pursue it and discover whether the person really does want to do these different things that may be offered to them.*

> *I've got a guy with an alcohol problem who got his order for a drink driving offence. It's only when you are three weeks into the order that you realise he is actually an alcoholic and that there are major problems that you haven't seen at the PSR stage.*

Drug users might be a classic example. They are motivated at the PSR stage, or maybe when they start an order. But then they relapse weeks or months down the line and the whole situation changes.

After court, then we have the battle of, you know, 'This is for real. What you were assessed to do before court is for real and now we have to implement it'.

During the time it takes to do a PSR you are only touching the surface and people are in these complex situations. The chaos will come out after the order has been made. In many ways you don't see the real person at the PSR stage because they are anxious to please, or usually they are anxious to get through court. It's when you get that sigh of relief that they are not going to prison that you can really get to the problems, so the supervision plan after six months may be totally different.

There is urgency to get things bolted down in the PSR, which over-simplifies what the process is all about.

Assessment says as much about the assessor as the assessed. [If someone else wrote the PSR] you may see things differently and have to get your head round it.

Post-sentence assessments for group referrals

While there are frequently delays before an offender begins attendance an a probation service group programme or before a place can be secured, there was not much evidence of referral decisions being made after a person had been placed on probation. In response to questions about criteria for referral to groups after supervision had commenced, many officers indicated that this was unlikely to happen except in the case of groups run by other agencies and groups where attendance is voluntary rather than subject to requirement. Even for in-house groups which combine voluntary and required attendance, the referral plans and arrangements had typically been made at the pre-sentence stage. As was indicated in Chapter 4, post-sentence applications to court, for additional attendance requirements to be inserted into a probation order, were unheard of:

In terms of having requirements the PSR is completely central. If the requirement is not built into the Order at that point, I know of no circumstance where an officer has gone back to Court and had it changed. It may be possible but it never happens.

However, in two county services, there were opportunities to assess the suit-ability of offenders for groups and community services after they have been made subject to a probation order.[7] In one of these services, new super-visees (unless in employment) were expected to attend an Induction Programme where an assessment was done over a period of three days, looking at issues such as employment, accommodation, relationships and substance abuse to determine what needs they have. It also provided infor-mation about groups and community resources. ("People are invited in who effectively advertise their wares, so you might invite the specialist alcohol worker from a local agency who then runs a slot to advertise their service".) In another county, the pre-sentence Assessment Project (described earlier in this chapter) had been extended for the purposes of post-sentence assess-ments in order to meet a county objective regarding assessment of employ-ment and training needs of offenders being supervised.

There were plans, in a third county, to run a 12-week Induction Programme. It was partly intended to help solve the problem of dealing with high caseloads while keeping to the parameters of the National Standards, but another aim was to "profile" supervisees more fully, identify areas of need with a view to setting up voluntary groups locally. It was intended that a supervising officer would be nominated for each offender, but during this 12-week period they would be seen in a group setting which team members co-lead. It was suggested by the SPO of this team that this model might be adopted county-wide.[8]

Systematic on-going assessment

Procedures, tools and consultation

Although probation staff regarded assessment and adjustments to the super-vision programme as a continuous process, the enterprise seemed to be largely a solo one, at least in 'straight' probation orders (those without requirements). Typically, there was little in the way of formalised procedures or input from others to monitor and assist on-going assessment and supervi-sion. Asked what systematic methods and tools are applied, the main responses concerned completion of supervision plans and quarterly review forms (36% POs; 58% SPOs) and the discussion and negotiation of such reviews and plans with the offender (45% POs; 48% SPOs). Team meetings were not often mentioned (nor supervision meetings with SPOs without prompting by the researcher), and very few officers said that checklists or

---

7   The information given here is limited to that obtained from the SPOs and POs in the field team: those directly
    involved in the projects described were not interviewed.
8   The schemes described here were regarded by interviewees as innovatory, though a few staff who had previously
    worked in other counties were aware of similar schemes elsewhere. Variously termed 'assessment projects', 'induc-
    tion groups', and 'in-take teams' (with some different but overlapping purposes) this approach has been adopted in
    several regions since the end of the seventies (Brown and Seymour, 1983). It was pioneered in Bristol in 1977
    (Weaver and Allum, 1993). Guidelines for practice have been set out by Brown and Burns (1983).

questionnaires were used as an aid to the assessment of needs; just ten staff altogether, including four from the same county:

> *When we start a case off these days we have to fill in quite a rigor-*
> *ous statistics sheet and we have to highlight what we feel the prob-*
> *lems are behind the offending… such as accommodation, employ-*
> *ment, lack of skills… A couple of months later our senior will be*
> *sent a sheet which shows how many of our cases have each of these*
> *problems. He will then chase us up and say 'Have you sent them to*
> *the Employment Liaison Scheme?'… It is a start to being more*
> *systematic.*

> *I'm not aware of anyone using questionnaires or tests. I mean*
> *nobody uses things like the repertory grid test, or questionnaires*
> *that would enable them to test and retest. We have something called*
> *a case-management form which begins to get at some of those*
> *issues, but we are still not at the point where people might use*
> *materials that they can keep using to demonstrate progress and*
> *change. The case-management form is supposed to be done jointly*
> *with offenders, so at least it does introduce some sort of self-assess-*
> *ment of the offender… But it does demand that people make some*
> *comment about whether areas have been discussed in relation to*
> *somebody's offending. And it then demands that they give some*
> *sort of professional judgement about the relationship between those*
> *features and a person's offending. And it is also supposed to be*
> *done in conjunction with the client so that it does invite some joint*
> *assessment.*

Supervision plans and review forms

In all services, supervision plans and quarterly reviews are part of supervi-sory procedure. These involve assessment of offenders' criminogenic and other needs, risks, and the appropriate action to take. Unless prompted, practitioners seldom identified these procedures as part of a systematic assessment process. Several areas have moved away from the blank page 'Part Bs' to pro-formas which structure the Supervision Plan and the subse-quent reviews. Some of these are still experimental. The more detailed and structured they are, the less officers seemed to like them. There was a wide-spread aversion to tick-box forms, sometimes articulated as resentment of a mechanical task which is done merely for the gratification of line-managers but which has no bearing on the quality of offender supervision. Such pro-formas appeared to be more acceptable if space was left – literally and metaphorically – for more descriptive evaluations and insights.

Meetings and consultations

In response to a question about what opportunities officers have to discuss their on-going supervision of offenders, the POs most often mentioned informal discussion with colleagues (86%) and, secondly, opportunities within supervision meetings with seniors (81%). Three-quarters of the SPOs referred to the informal help which officers provide for one another; and nine in ten mentioned supervision meetings with seniors. Other sources of input seen as contributing to assessment and supervision during the course of an order are shown in Table 5.4.

The majority of probation officers said they had monthly supervision meetings with their SPOs; meetings were more frequent with officers who were not yet accredited. Eleven officers had supervision meetings less often than monthly (including four who seldom met or who only met informally). Three-quarters of POs described supervision meetings as helpful, while a quarter had reservations – usually because of the limited time spent on the qualitative content of work:

> *We have the best SPO anyone could have, but there are more and more demands on him to focus on administrative detail.*

> *The meetings are too concerned with appraisal rather than my needs. The cases that get covered are the high risk ones – the ones that cover your back.*

> *If you get good supervision it is worth its weight in gold. I can remember [a previous senior] whose supervision was superb. It was so empowering and supportive... I am not criticising other seniors, because I believe [their] role is now ... a different role, and very difficult. It is almost 'undoable'.*

Table 5.4
POs opportunities for discussing supervision of offenders

	POs %	SPOs %
Informal discussion with colleagues	85.9	75.0
Supervision meetings with SPOs	80.8	90.0
Training courses (+ conferences)	34.6	50.0
Case discussion slot in meetings	12.8	17.5
Liaison with specialists	12.8	12.5
High risk[9] offenders case meetings	11.5	12.5
Meetings for case discussion only	6.4	12.5

A quarter of the SPOs were of the opinion that they were not doing enough to assist officers in their team with the task of carrying through supervision in the community. This was mainly because they were now charged with giving high priority to ensure that National Standards are being adhered to, and that all the correct procedures are being carried out for high risk offenders[10] and child protection cases; many were also having to manage much larger teams than previously. For some it was also because they were, by their own admission, out of touch with practice techniques and methods, and regarded the practitioners as more expert than themselves:

> In my supervision with Probation Officers, I look much more now at certain key pieces of information, ensuring that things have been done, as much as at what has been done. That makes me feel uncomfortable sometimes. When I look back at a supervision session and go to write up the notes, I find that a lot of it has been checking things and we haven't got into - what was covered when I started as a practitioner - the casework analysis bit. That marks for me a shift in my time in the probation service.

> One of the biggest question-marks that is around for the service at the moment is the role of the senior probation officer...when I picked up this job it wasn't like this and I certainly wouldn't

---

9   The 1992 National Standards stipulated that "the management of risk, both of serious reoffending and of serious harm to the public, where relevant, is an important part of the work of the service" and indicated ways of managing such risk (1992, chapter 3, para. 6). The 1995 National Standards stipulate that "In every case an assessment of the risk posed by the offender should be made. This should consider the risk to the public of reoffending or of causing serious harm (and its likely nature). Assessments should also consider the risk of self harm and risk to staff (1995, chapter 3, para. 6).

10   Despite this, in a recent HMIP investigation, it was found that "staff too often fail either to record or respond to indicators of potential dangerousness in offenders they supervise" (1995, para. 2.3, p.15) and that "Level of contact with offenders and enforcement of orders and licences indicate that [National Standards were not being complied with] in a significant number of cases, even where offenders are formally assessed as posing a risk to members of the public" (HM Inspectorate of Probation, 1995, para. 2.3, p.15).

apply for it now, I mean it is not what I would choose to do, but I am stuck in it at the moment. The role is much more about checking that people are doing what they are supposed to be doing.

In supervision meetings, what I talk about is how many reports have you done? How much slack have you got? Why didn't that happen? Can you do that on so and so? And it's very mechanical basic stuff. Very rarely do I talk about the content of supervision. What I did when I first came...I had a discussion with each member of staff about what supervision was...agreement about the nature of supervision. And certainly in the early days, I would go out with people and either watch them do work or occasionally co-work something... There was much more talking to people about what they were doing, reading about what they were doing, seeing how they got on in court... I was much more in tune... Now, only periodically do I even look at case records any more... The expectation of me is that I do do that as well as check that officers are doing things, but, quite honestly, its very difficult to carve out the chunk of time needed to check from two perspectives - first, that officers are doing things and keeping their records - and then getting a sense of the work they are doing.

My job is to set the boundaries, the parameters, the objectives of the casework; to impress upon staff that the overall purpose is to reduce offending. How officers do it is down to them, because they are the professional social workers. I see myself as a manager, not an in-depth caseworker.

Only two of the 40 teams visited were holding meetings specifically for the purpose of case discussion. A few said such case discussion meetings were planned or had been held in the past, and a quarter of the seniors said there was a slot or opportunity for case discussion in their general team meetings. In teams where there was no regular opportunity to discuss current cases in formalised meetings, almost all SPOs thought that it would be valuable to do this but doubted whether officers could find the necessary time. Eight in ten of the probation officers who were in teams without case discussion meetings said they would find such meetings valuable. Similarly, seven in ten thought a system of qualitatively reviewing each other's supervision work (comparable to gate-keeping of PSRs) would be advantageous. Most added, however, that they regarded such schemes as utopian, given staff cut-backs and the increasing demands being made of them.

Confidence and consistency in assessments

Accuracy of PSR assessment

More than half the POs (60%) regarded themselves as generally or usually able to make satisfactory PSR assessments (see Table 5.5): the rest acknowledged some fallibility on occasions, but this was mostly attributed to shortage of time for thorough investigation, or failing to tune in, and rarely to the difficulty of the task or insufficient tools or guidance:

> *I'm good at it... It comes from my life experiences, things that have happened in my life. There's something about theory in there, but I didn't know that until I went to college... I've always thought I'm very good at talking to people and engaging with people and being able to make assessments. It is partly about valuing people, respecting them.*

> *We assimilate a great deal of information in a very short span of time and can usually put our finger on what is going on in a person's life... It's a sixth sense, an awareness of what is going on... It is not always what you do. It is how you do it. If you are not empathic with that individual or if having a bad day and you rub each other up the wrong way, you are going to get very little information out of that person.*

> *What I have always tried to do is not to forget to operate at gut level to some extent. They are terribly important those feelings. There is a danger that you lose or suppress this, the more professional you become. I try not to. As a result, I hope I get a fairly good assessment of someone. It's about a feeling you get about someone when they are talking to you that you can't always encapsulate in words.*

Although several interviewees referred to assessment as partly instinctive, it may be that sometimes this is a mislabelling of an awareness of the changing dynamics of offending behaviour at different stages in criminal careers:

> *Part of it is instinct. You come across someone who has got 15 previous. They have been in and out many, many times. They have failed probation, failed community service, no hope. But they come in and sit down and you are going to go through the process again. All of a sudden something will go BOING. They have come to a part of their life where there is that eye, an opening – just that little bit there – a realisation that they have got something to lose for the first time – a partner, a job. You can cut through all the bull that*

*they have been through before and you can get through to them. So
I don't think that you have got to be too cynical, although you do
need a degree of cynicism as some protection. That's part of the
process of analysing where people are at. It's not all about what
their past is, or what the offence is - it's where they are in this
continuum. [SPO]*

Many of the seniors, like practitioners, were confident (57%) in officers'
ability to cope well with this task. However, one in five of the seniors, in
contrast to only one of the practitioners, regarded the assessment process as
too unsystematic and in need of refinement.

This perhaps reflects SPO's greater experience of evaluating PSRs and their
awareness from a management perspective of the potential for more systematic assessment.

Table 5.5
Views on accuracy of PSR assessment

Are you / your POs good at PSR assessment?	*PO* %	*SPO* %
Generally/usually accurate	60.5	56.7
Varies due to time limits	26.3	13.5
Varies (author factors)	9.2	2.7
Varies (defendant factors)	3.9	10.8
Process too crude	1.3	21.6

Consistency between PSR writers

While most officers seemed to be confident in the quality of their court
reports (including those who admitted to sometimes being wrong in their
PSR assessments of the offenders),[11] there was less confidence in consistency
of content and sentencing proposals. That is, when asked if the content and
proposal in a report was likely to be the same regardless of who wrote the
report, over half (57% POs and 58% SPOs) thought that there were likely to
be differences. However, this still leaves four in ten who were either very
confident that there would be consistency regardless of the writer, or satisfied that such differences would be slight or exceptional. Potential inconsistencies were attributed to differences in professional experience, in officer

---

11   'Gate-keeping' and quality control procedures are particularly concerned with the relevance of content and the
      avoidance of discriminatory comments and stereotyping.

specialisms and interests, in assessment skill and, sometimes unavoidably, to varying perceptions and interpretations:

> *Different people see different things and different ways of doing things. When one is in court with PSRs one reads through them and thinks "I wouldn't have gone for that option, I would have gone for this". It does vary. An officer might propose community service where I would have proposed probation.*

> *If someone is doing a lot of work with alcohol, or if someone knows a lot about substance abuse they will perhaps ask questions that they wouldn't if they weren't so aware. Or if they were very conscious about domestic violence, they are going to be looking at those things. That's the subjective bit. I don't believe you will ever get rid of that – we are not robotic.*

> *You do bring your own slant to things... I can remember one of the clerical officers in a previous team where I worked saying "It's funny. When I type your cases up they have all got family problems, and when I type up [_____'s] they have all got health problems".*

Consistency in supervision

Far fewer thought that the content of supervision would be the same irrespective of who the supervising officer was. Only three of the POs and two of the SPOs claimed this. One in ten of the officers felt they were not in a position to answer the question, but altogether 95% of seniors and 85% of practitioners thought there would be differences in the way that a supervision programme was conducted depending on which officer was assigned the job. Numerous reasons were given for potential variations, but the principal ones were:

Table 5.6
Why supervision varies depending on officer

(Multiple responses)	All %	POs %	SPOs %
Officer style, personality, approach	63.1	61.5	65.8
Choice of methods/techniques/referrals	59.2	60.0	57.9
Offender-officer rapport/fit	22.3	23.1	21.1

Successful completion of supervision

The interviewees[12] were asked about 'what works'; that is, which factors they regarded as most crucial to whether the goals of a supervision programme were achieved: officer factors (e.g. skills, approach), offender factors (e.g. motivation, social circumstances), resource factors (e.g. staff shortage, groups available), sentencing factors (e.g. information to sentencers, severity of sentence). One in ten POs and two in ten SPOs said all of these could be relevant, either in interaction or at different times and in different cases. The remaining officers identified one or more of the factors listed in Table 5.7 as the most critical. However, as may be seen in the table, there was a difference between the views of practitioners and seniors. POs were more likely to select offender factors, while SPOs were more likely to pick out officers as the key variable.

Table 5.7
Effective supervision: the most critical factor(s)

	All n=77 %	POs n=48 %	SPOs n=29 %
Offender factors	53.2	60.4	41.4
Officer factors	40.3	33.3	51.7
Officer-offender relationship	22.1	27.1	13.8
Resource factors	20.8	25.0	13.8
Sentence/PSR-stage factors	20.8	18.8	24.1
Interaction/can't say/it varies	14.3	10.4	20.7

The references to offender factors were mainly concerned with whether or not the offender presented problems which got in the way of a supervision plan for reducing reoffending. Thus, attributions to offenders were more often negative than positive, and correspond to those mentioned as obstacles to effective supervision (therefore, see next paragraph for illustrations of the 'offender factor'). Seniors were more likely to draw a contrast between the abilities of different officers, while the POs tended to minimise or negate the relevance of such differences:

---

12 This was one of the final questions addressed, and unfortunately was omitted from a third of the interviews when time had run out. However, a related question, concerned with obstacles to the effectiveness of supervision, was discussed with all the interviewees, and provided similar information (see next paragraph).

Officer factor

It depends a lot on the professionalism of the officer... When you get a breakdown of who is referring to the probation centre you find that some hardly ever refer and some refer a lot... Probation officers do exercise an awful lot of power in choosing what to offer. It's one of the main equal opportunities to be addressed. [SPO]

Quite a lot of the work is very much intuitive and is hard to quantify... Whereas we want officers to operate to a good standard of work with every single defendant and client, we want to give everybody the same bite of the cherry, if it is too prescriptive, it will cut down on some fairly ingenious work that can take place between a probation officer and client, and I think it would be sad if we lost that. [SPO]

Nobody has all the answers and I don't know that there is a right path for any of our clients. There isn't just one way to get to the point where they don't reoffend. The quality of service that clients receive is always the same, even if the approach varies. [PO]

Officer-offender relationship

I am a human being too. Sometimes I give better service to one offender than another. Maybe one offender strikes a chord with me and I go to endless effort. A lot of the contacts will be routine but periodically I will really pull the stops out and let no obstacles get in the way. I suddenly see that this is what you have to go for... Sometimes I have had a case that is pretty negative and I am getting nowhere. An option we don't consider is would it all come to life if it was transferred to another colleague. [PO]

There's a part of me that's a bit old-fashioned and believes that there is something potentially significant in the strength of the relationship which has developed between an officer and his or her client... It's a kind of mentor role that I think is quite important. [SPO]

Obstacles to effectiveness

The most frequently identified obstacles to doing effective work with a person subject to supervision were: offenders' lack of motivation to stop offending and to co-operate with the supervision plan (41%); offenders' incapacity to co-operate adequately with the supervision plan – e.g. because of mental illness, learning difficulties, drug addiction or chaotic lifestyle (34%); unemployment or material and financial hardship (27%); and pressure of work and insufficient time to get through all that is expected and necessary (41%).

Offender factor

[The main obstacle is] the difference in clients' attitude pre-court to their attitude once they are on probation. Not always, but often, it's 'Yes I'll do anything you say so long as I don't go to prison' and you meet the same person a week after they've been to court, and it's like they've transformed... What you get then is 'We talked about your alcohol problems and how that led to this assault ...' and they are saying 'Ah, yeah, well, I haven't had a drink for weeks now and that's not a problem any more' and 'well, I've learnt my lesson now...' and it's like it's all been taken away. And you are left saying 'I was talking to you two weeks ago and you admitted then you'd need help with this problem...'. But it is brushed aside, and you are left stuck with this barrier.

He's a good example of someone it's difficult to work with because, even though he's not unco-operative, he doesn't engage at all. It's about motivation. Getting people motivated to do things is a big problem – especially the younger ones or the more immature ones.

How can you talk meaningfully to someone about offending if they haven't got a roof over their head or if they haven't got a hope of improving their income?

If you stick to the supervision plan regardless, you are going to lose the client – 'cos they are more interested in, say, why the DHSS had their benefit book taken from them. You have to deal with practical problems first. DHSS may well have made a mistake... You should have supervision plans yes, but they are not the Bible.

Time factor

Lack of time is the main obstacle – especially when there are a lot of reports: the clients go by the wayside! We joke about it, but it's not funny really. It is the reality at times.

We need to be realistic about what we can do in the time available... You work in depth in a minority of cases. New officers can give more time... Magistrates think we've got oceans of time. It's not the case. You haven't got the space to see clients when problems come up. No time for home visits. Loads of paperwork to do: all the case records, all the reports. You're probably working effectively with just five or six of your cases.

It would appear that there are some differences between seniors' and practitioners' estimation of these problems. Proportionally more of the seniors mentioned pressure of work as a main obstacle,[13] while offender factors were more frequently mentioned by POs:

Table 5.8
Obstacles to effective supervision

	POs %	SPOs %
Offender motivation to co-operate	45.6	31.4
Offender capacity to co-operate	41.2	20.0
Pressure of work/insufficient time	36.8	48.4
Unemployment/financial hardship	29.4	22.9
Probation/community resources	8.8	17.1

The relatively low proportion (especially in the case of POs) mentioning gaps in or inadequate probation service or community resources as a barrier indicated that there is no strong association between offenders' poor progress while on community supervision and lack of resources, in the sense of in-house provision such as groups and specialists (as opposed to number of staff and staff time).

---

13   However, at some point during the interviews nearly all of the practitioners mentioned a sense of being overloaded (with large caseloads, report preparation, excessive paperwork).

6 Improving offender-programme matching

Summary of key findings

Criteria for assignment of work

Interviewees described various systems for the assignment of pre-sentence reports (PSRs) and of supervision, ranging from allocation meetings, in which practitioners are consulted and put in bids, to a more mechanistic process of assignment on a rota basis or workload basis. The extent to which SPOs took on the responsibility for assigning reports and cases varied. There was sometimes a principal criterion for assignment (such as the area in which the defendant resided) but often several factors were balanced and weighted depending on the case and professional needs at the time. Size and equity of officers' workload was virtually always an issue which could sway the final decision, while some teams prioritised the avoidance of delay, and others the continuity of an officer's involvement in any one case. Attention was given, to some extent, to practitioners' interests and specialisms, but it was only in particular types of work that this ever took precedence (e.g. sex offenders, female offenders).

Alternative assignment systems

It was generally acknowledged that allocation meetings were time-consuming and a cause of delay, though practitioners appreciated opportunities to have their preferences and interests taken into account. One system for assigning PSRs which was strongly praised for its expediency was a recently introduced arrangement whereby a pre-scheduled timetable for PSR preparation enabled appointments to be fixed immediately after adjournment for reports. Although that system did not allow for considerations about matching offenders to officer's interests and preferences, on the plus side, practitioners found that it helped them rationalise their time because of the advance structure imposed and the enhanced control over time resulting from a decrease in unkept PSR appointments.

Specialist PSR preparation

When it came to allocating probation and supervision orders, in most areas there was a presumption in favour of PSR writers becoming supervisors. It was argued that the supervising officer was disadvantaged in teams where there were officers with the specialist function of preparing reports. The rationale given for this is that the run-up period prior to appearing in court and being sentenced is especially opportune for forming a supervisory relationship because of the offender's motivation to avoid further court appearances and to negotiate a plan leading to change. There is no doubt that this is part of many officers' experience and that some form of supervisory 'bonding' occurs in a proportion of cases: four in ten said the PSR stage was critical for offender engagement with the supervisor. However, many of the same officers presented the paradox that the constraints and pressures on the defendant at that time are such that a false or limited picture is likely to be obtained. Examples of unsatisfactory assessment and planning at the PSR stage were given and in one area with a fairly well-established system of specialism (PSR writing and responsibility for supervision being largely separate functions) the SPOs, in particular, disputed that PSR writers who became supervisors began with a head-start.

Typical supervision practice

One-to-one work with offenders was at the core of supervision programmes in all ten of the areas studied: that is, the offender reported to his or her supervisor at the probation office, and plans and progress were discussed. Many officers made use of exercises and tasks and employed methods which are used in group programmes (such as role-playing). Typical practice consisted of working from a supervision plan, which was drafted at the PSR stage and which was negotiated and shared with the offender and then reviewed on a quarterly basis. Referrals to groups, specialists and to community resources were frequently part of that plan, although if there were no requirements written into the court order, there was considerable variation in how much the supervision concentrated on the one-to-one work; some officers were much more active than others in making such referrals and in facilitating offenders' use of resources.

Offender assessment and allocation

The complex and time-consuming task of offender assessment and allocation was typically done by probation officers (POs), with checks, consultation and referrals for additional assessments being largely a matter for their discretion. Assessment activities were mostly concentrated at the PSR stage (not surprisingly, given that this is a purpose of the report). However, assessment is described as continuing throughout the order, with supervision plans being reviewed on a quarterly basis, in consultation with the offender. Most teams had some form of PSR gate-keeping or quality control procedure whereby colleagues were consulted about the content of reports. Areas varied in their assessment policies for groupwork requirements: in some places, group-workers made the assessment, but in others the decision about suitability was left to the report writer. Once an order of supervision had been imposed, assessment was even more of a lone activity: in most services, and in most cases, there was little by way of formal input from colleagues and other agencies to aid assessment and ongoing supervision, apart from some space found for this in formal meetings with seniors (SPOs).

A more thorough offender assessment was made in some cases. Pre-sentence reports on sex offenders were based on more interviews than was typical, and sometimes co-workers are assigned to prepare the PSRs, and to super-vise sex offenders. There were regulations about the checks which should be made where there may be child protection issues. Assessment meetings and additional oversight were more likely in the case of offenders who had been identified as of high risk to the public.[1]

There were a number of service variations – usually minor but occasionally major – which are likely to increase the use of groups and other resources:

- precise county objectives, or targets, for use of resources (groups, hostels, volunteers, etc.)

- group-workers or specialist visits to team meetings (to publicise their activities)

- PO involvement in co-leading the groups.

These are likely to result in more referrals and more use of resources, princi-pally by concentrating the mind of officers when they are making assess-ments.

Reasons for referrals

Referrals were more likely to be made if the group programme or specialist resource could be clearly seen to meet the individual's offence-related needs. A critical factor was whether officers knew enough about the resource to make a judgement about its potential usefulness. Therefore, publicity, good liaison and feedback, and experience of co-leading the programme, were all contribu-tory to whether or not an attendance proposal or referral had been made.

---

1   See Footnote 9 in chapter 5.

Equally, a better knowledge of the resource, a good reputation and specificity of purpose, each made it easier to 'sell' the programme to offenders.

Reasons for under-use of groups and other facilities

The most frequently mentioned reasons for not proposing referrals to group programmes were: (a) doubts about whether the offender could realistically be expected to keep up with the attendance requirement; and (b) uncertainties about the suitability of the group or facility for the offender (for example, if the content was seen as too broad and therefore much of it not relevant to that individual; or if the content was seen as too educational and impersonal). Where breach proceedings could result, officers played safe by not "setting up clients to fail".

Variability in supervision practice

Although 'gate-keeping' (checks and quality control) at the PSR stage, and meetings with the SPO while the order is in progress, are likely to systematise decisions to some extent, these procedures are themselves not standardised. And the National Standards for supervising offenders are regarded as having affected the timing and quantity of contact rather than the content of the programmes. Therefore, variations in the content of supervision will arise, at least partly, from unsystematic, arbitrary differences. Indeed, most of the interviewees believed that the supervision programme for any one offender is likely to vary according to which officer becomes their supervisor, whether because of differences of personal style and approach, different choices of methods and resources, or because officer and offender establish a good rapport.

Systems to improve assessment and matching

Other arrangements which affected the way offenders were allocated included:

*   automatic pre-sentence assessment for suitability to attend a group programme (for defendants above a specified seriousness band)

*   pre-sentence assessment programme (for unemployed defendants)

*   post-sentence induction and assessment programmes
    (for new probationers).

In one area, there was a procedure for all defendants who were unemployed to be referred to the probation centre for assessment by specialists, and the additional information was fed-back to the PSR writers. In three[2] counties (in one or more of the teams), post-sentence induction and assessment had been introduced.[3] Offenders were referred to a centre where they were able to find out for themselves about the resources on offer, and where there was further assessment from other probation staff and partnership staff. In some areas, if the offence was within a specified band of seriousness, the defendant would automatically be referred to be assessed for the probation centre programme. In each of these instances, because there was an obligatory or recommended referral, reliance on the judgement of the assigned officer was avoided to some extent, and the offenders were more actively included in the assessment and allocation process.

Some implications and recommendations

These findings are derived primarily from the perspectives of practitioners and their immediate managers: those who are most directly responsible for assessment and supervision. While it is clear that this focus was both appropriate and necessary, a more comprehensive investigation of these issues should also include the perspectives of sentencers, offenders, and of group-workers and higher management staff. Further discussion within the probation service should take place before drawing definitive policy implications. However, the data gathered for this study suggest some avenues towards the improvement of offender assessment and allocation.

Whether or not offenders placed on probation are disadvantaged by being assigned to a supervisor who was not the PSR writer is not an easy question to resolve. There are strong arguments on both sides, which are in turn complicated by other organisational variations – in particular, the extent to which others are involved in assessing the offender pre-sentence, and whether the supervision will comprise largely one-to-one work or whether there will be co-working, or referral to groups and others.

If the quality of supervision is disadvantaged by separating PSR writing and supervision, then the choice of PSR writer should be made with the prospect of supervision in mind, and with consideration to matching (for instance, whether the supervisor's style matches the offender's learning style; whether the officer has adequate specialist knowledge; whether the officer has any difficulty supervising this kind of offender). On a practical level, regardless of whether or not there is continuity in any one case, it seems appropriate for practitioners to be experienced in both PSR preparation and supervision so that the work they do at one stage has regard

2   In one case, it had not yet been put into operation but was scheduled to begin within the next few months.
3   Similar schemes have been applied in probation services not included in this study. See Footnote 8 in chapter 5.

to the work done at the other. If the functions are split, a supervising officer is more likely to appreciate the limitations of a "cold" PSR assessment (i.e. defendant is unknown) while, as emphasised by Lacey:

> ...*much depends on the quality of [PSR] assessment. It is the core skill which underpins all probation work and should be undertaken by the most skilled and experienced practitioners who have already had extensive experience of supervising people on probation orders. It is quite strange how the Service allows this task to be undertaken by students... (1995, p.18)*

The extent to which the PSR stage may be a valuable opportunity for beginning an interventionist relationship with a prospective probationer may be outweighed by other issues or may not be very important in the long-term as: any such advantages may be only transitory and of little comparative relevance, for example, six months into the order; second, in so far as officer to offender matching might be important (see Andrews, 1995), there is less chance of achieving this at the pre-sentence stage when the person is relatively unknown; and third, in an area where there are pre-sentence assessment centres or post-sentence induction programmes or intake teams, the individual officer becomes one element in a multi-faceted programme and so arguments for continuity are diluted. There are indications that the functional division facilitates the speed of report preparation, making it more feasible to work to court time limits. Without a broader survey which includes the perspectives of higher management and specialist PSR writers, it is premature to conclude firmly that a separation of the PSR writing function from the supervisory function is better practice; but, in the absence of lasting advantages to be claimed for report-to-order continuity, the possible streamlining of the system to avoid delays and cut down on administration becomes attractive.

In the words of one officer: "offender assessment is an inexact science" and, as one senior said, it is "a crude process". Probation staff are only allowed a short period of time for the completion of a PSR assessment, and in the majority of cases there is heavy reliance on one or two interviews with the defendant. The amount of checking, further inquiries and consultation of others is (subject to the consent of the defendant) left to the discretion of the officer, who is likely to be faced with other pressing priorities. It was evident from case material examined in this project that relevant information is often not discovered until after supervision has commenced. There is scope for additional input into assessment, before sentence or immediately following sentence, and also on a continuing basis throughout the period when the order is in force.

A more systematic assessment of offending-related needs will enhance the accuracy and status of probation assessments, will foster optimum use of in-house and partnership specialists, and would facilitate integrated evaluation of the effectiveness of community supervision. As Roberts has argued:

There is a clear need for the use of more rigorous and systematic forms of assessment, possibly making greater use of well-validated schedules and tests, and thereby ensuring that the individual idiosyncrasies of practitioners are reduced to the minimum" (1995, pp.225-226).

In addition to use of validated tests, other ways in which assessment could be made more systematic might include: provision of procedural assistance in gaining the defendant's consent so that more consultations and verifications can be made; explicit referral policies for each group and partnership arrangement; and guidance on the circumstances in which such referrals should be made (for instance, one of the services in this study made use of algorithms to assist in targeting people for the group programmes). There are various procedures increasingly in use or being considered, which seemed likely to benefit assessment and the tailoring of supervision: printed assessment guides and frameworks; structured supervision plan forms and quarterly review forms; resource directories and data bases available to each team. Each of these seems worthy of attention in services where they have not yet been applied.

'Pre-sentence assessment projects' and 'post-sentence induction programmes' seem particularly worthy of further attention and investigation. Both systems involve referral of the offenders to a centre, where assessment is facilitated by visiting specialists and group-workers, and they are acquainted with probation centre activities. Feedback from both has been encouraging. In the case of the pre-sentence assessment it was positive comments from the defendants which helped turn what was a pilot project into established practice. The group assessment and induction programmes are not novel to the probation service as a whole (see Brown and Seymour, 1983)[4] but in the areas visited, they were either experimental or only recently established. The outcomes will be of interest within the probation service, with a view to whether they could usefully be adopted more widely. Although it is now common practice for a supervision plan to be written into the PSR, the recent reduction in the time available for a PSR to be prepared, makes a post-sentence induction scheme even more valid. As pointed out by Roberts:

While the broad parameters of a disposal will already have been determined by the court... there is almost always still considerable

---

[4] Although induction programmes (otherwise known as "assessment groups", "in-take teams", "foundation" and "orientation groups") have been around in some probation services fro some time, such systems have perhaps come of age in this modern era of multi-dimensional community supervision.

discretion in the allocation to and provision of different programmes within a sentence... so at this stage it should be possible for a thorough assessment to be undertaken of each individual offender. (1995, p.225)

Regardless of how skilled, competent or well-trained, it could be argued that the individual practitioner is left to shoulder too much of the responsibility for on-going assessment and supervision of offenders. This seems especially true post-sentence, because pre-sentence assessment has generally benefitted from colleagues' insights and knowledge of resources shared through the forum of systematic gate-keeping or quality control systems. There was usually less routine discussion to support on-going assessment and allocation throughout an order: scarcely any teams had purpose-specific case-discussion meetings. Supervision meetings with seniors provided a valued but limited opportunity to address the decisions being made with selected cases. More often, there was unscheduled case discussion which took place in staff-rooms, and via informal consultation between colleagues. Practitioners were mutually supportive and accessible, and therefore generally did not feel isolated, but they may be relying too much on each others' judgement and advice at the expense of other important sources of information. There was an admission by many in this study that the offender, as the consumer of supervisory practice, receives variable provision depending on which officer is assigned as supervisor. Scheduled case discussion meetings would help guard against discriminatory supervision, would facilitate the sharing of skills, knowledge and responsibility, and would make joint consultation a formal requirement. The gains and rewards which have been claimed for quality control discussions of pre-sentence reports, indicate that formal meetings to consider current supervisory work would be profitable, and appreciated so long as there is an appropriate time dispensation.

There was considerable variability in the extent to which senior officers guided, assisted with and evaluated supervision practice, and in the parts they played in setting up procedures to support community supervision. Some felt increasingly cut off from the techniques and theories of offender supervision. Some seemed more active than others in facilitating meetings, providing information, monitoring and encouraging resource use, and in helping officers adjust to what is frequently termed a 'culture change' within the service. The shift in the nature of SPOs' work, over recent years, to a greater management role, and the substantial demands this makes of them, did not allow them, many felt, to make a sufficient contribution to ensuring the quality of supervision. A review of the role of SPOs would help to clarify what their role should be.

The advantages and disadvantages of voluntary versus required attendance on group programmes should be researched to find out about the relative referral rates, and the relative attendance and completion rates, and the effects of attendance rules on programme integrity and outcome. The referral criteria for use of group programmes, particularly the more intensive 1A(3) programmes, present officers with a 'Catch 22' situation. These programmes are intended for offenders whose level and pattern of offending and whose very problems (poor anger management, alcohol abuse, entrenched criminality and the chaotic lifestyle which goes with it) make them seem less able to reliably attend. Paradoxically, these restrictive and demanding programmes are intended for offenders whose entrenched behaviour problems mean that officers will hesitate to say that they will conform to the regime. Similarly, there may be little confidence that the offender, even if attending, will respond to the programme. Yet it may be that, because of their learning styles, those people who raise such doubts will respond better to the structured and activity-based programme of a group, than they would to a 'straight' probation order (see Andrews, 1995). In considering appropriate court disposals, probation officers and sentencers need to be well-informed about research findings on 'what works' so that offenders of suitable 'risk classification', 'responsivity', etc. (McGuire and Priestley, 1995) can be appropriately targeted.

The Chief Inspector of the Probation Service has emphasised that, while the service "faces increased financial control ... and a relentless drive for increased output and effectiveness", one of its responsibilities is to "offer value for money to the community at large" (Smith, 1995). On the simple basis of staff-to-offender ratio it has to be acknowledged that groups are likely to be better value for money than one-to-one supervision, providing, of course, that the outcomes are shown to be at least equally as effective, and providing they are not under-used (potentially resulting in an uneconomical ratio of staff to offenders). In so far as there is some resistance, or at least reservation, on the part of probation staff to the growth of groupwork programmes and partnership arrangements, where necessary, steps should be taken to overcome problems and barriers, and to allay staff concerns. For instance, ensuring that adequate transport arrangements are available for offenders living at a distance from places where groups are held is essential. There should be clear referral policies, which are also made known to sentencers; there should be realistic expectations regarding breach and enforcement. Officers want to give probationers the best chance of getting through their orders without breaching them (that is, to avoid "setting them up to fail"), and where there is insufficient information about a facility, or doubt about its relevance to the probationer, they "play safe" by not making a referral. Therefore, ensuring that POs are knowledgeable about effective resources, are kept fully informed about the progress of probationers, and have opportunities to attend and co-lead groups, should lead to more referrals.

Recent moves within the probation service have given increasing emphasis to alternative ways of working with offenders (groups, partnerships, referrals to other agencies), and research on 'what works' indicate these are to be welcomed as likely to advance the effectiveness of supervision. However, many of the POs expressed concern that the expansion of their responsibilities as case-managers will gradually squeeze out their key role as professionals working directly with individual probationers to bring about change. The SPOs, most of whom supported the move towards case-management, confirmed that such misgivings were common amongst practitioners.

In the view of this researcher, there is a danger of "throwing the baby out with the bath water" if one-to-one work is not also developed alongside groupwork and the involvement of other agencies, and its efficacy systematically examined along with the value of other approaches. While the quality of much one-to-one work in the service may have left room for improvement, the standard of previous practice is not a reason for devaluing the method itself. There are several reasons why it might be more appropriate to promote and improve one-to-one work.[5] (1) Work on an individual level is the link between all other modes of intervention. (2) Most of the ingredients identified as relevant to effective supervision programmes (such as structure, focus on offending, programme integrity, multi-modality – see McGuire, 1995) are equally applicable to one-to-one work. (3) And while group programmes have some benefits which by definition are absent from one-to-one settings, the reverse also applies. That is, a one-to-one programme may better match a probationer's learning style, if for instance, the individual is detached, uncomfortable or disruptive in a group setting. (4) Also, quite simply – just as in the context of other personal and social relationships – there is an improved chance of getting to know the offender in a one-to-one rather than group setting, thereby facilitating assessment and tailoring to the offender's needs. (5) Finally, there is a wealth of experience and research which demonstrates the validity of one-to-one therapeutic or counselling relationships as powerful vehicles for changing behaviour (e.g. Egan, 1985; Oldfield, 1987), and it is most unlikely that none of this has applicability for offenders. Whether or not there are elements of the supervisory relationship, distinguishable from the methods used, which are as instrumental in achieving the aims of supervision is a question which would merit closer investigation. Certainly such a view is embedded with the roots of the probation service and it is clear that many probation staff continue to regard the "relationship factor" as critical (e.g. Bailey, 1995). In a fairly recent survey undertaken for the New Zealand Department of Justice, it was found that:

---

5   It should be stressed that this is in no way an argument for a return to traditional one-to-one work by itself, and without any reference to the group programmes and partnership arrangements which have greatly enhanced the potential of supervision in the community, and have added important new dimensions to the work of the probation service in reducing crime.

The nature of the relationship between the Probation Officer and client was thought to be the pivotal factor in influencing offending behaviour. Both management and field staff believed that if the relationship is good... then it opens the door to influence – which in turn means that the client is more likely to look at the options offered and may choose not to reoffend. This appears to be the most powerful underlying rationale for why Probation does what it does and believes it can sometimes contribute to a reduction in reoffending. (Leibrich, 1991, p46)

In this exploratory study it was possible to identify some patterns and distinctions in the practice of offender assessment and allocation: a larger-scale survey would be necessary to distinguish how these are linked to the effectiveness of supervision. It is self-evident that this study was not an investigation into the effectiveness of various modes of intervention, but it did help throw into relief the variable content of one-to-one work (as indicated in views about officer autonomy and lack of consistency between supervision practice on an individual level). Recent analyses of research on "what works" have given rise to more optimism than was possible one to two decades ago, but much more, and better, "what works" research is needed; and research and evaluation systems must be integrated into the provision of supervision programmes (as has been advocated by Sheldon, 1987; by Roberts, 1995, and many others). There is a need for more communication across probation service areas, so that the benefits and lessons of experimental and innovative systems can be shared.

Appendix: main questions covered in interviews

Interview of probation officers

A – Nature and purpose of supervision in the community

A1. When an offender is placed on probation, what, in your view, should the goal or purpose of the supervising officer be?

A2. Do you see your view of the purpose(s) of a probation order as in agreement with the official purposes as set out in National Standards and probation service statements of purpose?

    A2i. [If different] In what respect are official standards/ purpose(s) different?

A3. Is it possible for you to put into a nutshell the main means by which you work with offenders to reduce the risk of their reoffending?

A4. What is your view of the introduction of standardisation into probation officers work (that is, the principle of standardisation as distinct from the content of the National Standards)?

    A4i. What is your view of National Standards in practice?

A5. What is your view of more detailed monitoring and recording of work done with offenders?

A6. What is your view of the increased emphasis, in the probation service on working in partnership with other bodies and services in the community?

    A6i. Why in favour?

    A6ii. Why against?

A7. Of the various modes of working with offenders – one-to-one work, groupwork, the PO as case-manager making appropriate referrals – which in your view tends to be most effective, or which mode of working should be the most dominant?

B – One-to-one work

B1. Apart from general discussion and talking to them, what different techniques, procedures or materials do you frequently use in your one-to-one work with offenders?

B2. Is there any particular counselling or psychological approach which you tend to adopt in your one-to-one work (such as a psychodynamic approach, or a cognitive-behavioural approach)?

B3. Do you home visit your clients (over and above the minimum requirement)?

B3i What is the value of home visits?

B4. Do you make use of volunteers?

B4i. What's your view of the value of volunteers?

B5. To what extent do you feel you have autonomy to decide on how to work with offenders, once they are placed on probation?

B5i. Should officers have autonomy and discretion (regarding referrals, methods, approach etc? [i.e. after confirmed].

B6. At the PSR stage, what is your criteria for referring an offender to attend a group? That is, at the PSR stage, what would lead you to recommend a probation order with conditions to attend a programme, as opposed to a straight probation order?

B6i. Can offenders be referred onto programmes on a voluntary basis?

B6ii. What about referral once an order has been made – what would be the basis for referring an offender then?

B7. Do you have any reservations in general about referring offenders for groupwork ?

B8. Once you have made a referral what, if anything, do you frequently do to support or facilitate their attendance?

C – Allocation to programmes and resources

C1. What's your view of the resources in this county for working with offenders? First, the provision by the Probation Service itself – Would you say that the overall provision is good or not?
(a) in-house (b) partnership and community

C2. Are there any important gaps, or shortfalls in provision – either in-house, or in local community?

C3. What are the main strengths in your area – whether county-wide or local provision?

C4. Are there any groups or resources which are particularly favoured for referrals/favoured by you?

C4i. [If any] (a) Which? (b) Why?

C5. Do you feel you are sufficiently well-informed about resources in this area?

C5i. [If not well-informed] Why not?

C6. Do you feel you make full use of the resources which are available to you in this area?

C7. Are there groups or resources which get under-used or which you are reluctant to use, or uneasy about using? (including lapsed/defunct)

C7i. [If any] (a) Which? (b) Why?

D – Allocation to supervising officer

D1. Do you know on what basis PSRs are allocated to you?

D1i. Which is the predominant factor?

D2. Do you know on what basis offenders are allocated to you for supervision?

D2i. Which is the predominant factor?

D3. Do you think the allocation system could be improved?

D3i. [If yes] How? – what should allocation depend on?

E – Assessment

E1. What is being assessed at the PSR stage? (There is quite a range of issues being explored and questions being asked – can you run through them?)

E2. What are you using to help you make these PSR assessments? Where is all that information coming from?

E2i People?

E2ii Records?

E2iii Tools/Guides?

E3. Are there any referrals you are required to make for the purpose of assessment (whether at the PSR stage or later)?

E4. Do you use any guidelines or framework to help you decide what to assess and how to go about assessment at the PSR stage or later?

E5 What [other] systematic procedures or checks are followed routinely/ regularly in attempting to match the offender to programmes or forms of intervention [apart from required referrals, as mentioned in qE3] ?

E6. What system do you have for PSR gate-keeping/monitoring? (e.g. rota? duty officer?)

E6i. Is this system satisfactory?

E6ii. Do you find the gate-keeping helpful?

E7. How critical is the PSR stage? [And, if so why?]

E8. Are you good at making offender assessments at the PSR stage (and deciding on a suitable intervention or supervision plan)?

E9. When supervising an offender, are you likely to make a re-assessment/ new plan (one which is different from that at the PSR stage?)

E10. Once someone is on probation to you, what opportunities are there for further assessment, and discussing the content of supervision?

E11. How often do you have supervision meetings with your SPO?

E11i. Do you find supervision sessions with your SPO helpful?

E12. Would you find it helpful to have case-discussion in team meetings?

E13. Would you find it helpful to have a quality control/monitoring procedure concerned with content of supervision?

E14. Is there any means by which you think assessment procedures can be improved?

F – Equality and effectiveness

F1. Would the PSR content be pretty much the same (including the proposal) regardless of who the PSR writer was?

F1i. [If no, or occasional differences] Why might it differ?

F2. Would an offender get the same supervision programme (i.e. forms of intervention, methods, referrals) regardless of who the supervising officer was?

F2i. [If no, or occasional differences] Why might the programme differ?

F3. There is probably an interplay of factors which influence the effectiveness of a programme of supervision: there are sentencing factors (like how demanding the sentence is), there are officer factors (such as skills, methods), there are offender factors (such as motivation to change) and there are resources factors (what groups and services are available). Thinking about what works in reducing offending, would you say that any of these are more crucial than others?

F3i. [If issues at pre-sentence/sentencing stage] Which sentencing factors make a difference?

F3ii. [If officer factors] Which officer factors make a difference?

F3iii.[If offender factors] Which offender factors make a difference?

F3iv. [If resource factors] Which resource factors make a difference?

F3v. [If policy/practice factors] Which policy/practice factors make a difference?

F4. Once somebody is the subject of a probation order, what, in your experience, are the main obstacles to doing effective work with them?

F5. What aspect of the work gives you your job satisfaction?

Interview of senior officers

A – Nature and purpose of supervision in the community

A1. When an offender is placed on probation, what, in your view, should the goal or purpose of the supervising officer be?

A2. Do you see your view of the purpose(s) of a probation order as in agreement with the official purposes as set out in National Standards and probation service statements of purpose?

A2i. [If different] In what respect are official standards/purpose(s) different?

A3. Is it possible for you to put into a nutshell the main means by which officers work with offenders to reduce the risk of their reoffending?

A4. What is your view of the introduction of standardisation into probation officers work (that is, the principle of standardisation as distinct from the content of the National Standards)?

A4i. What is your view of National Standards in practice?

A5. What is your view of more detailed monitoring and recording of work done with offenders?

A6. What is your view of the increased emphasis, in the probation service on working in partnership with other bodies and services in the community?

A6i. Why in favour?

A6ii. Why against?

A7. Of the various modes of working with offenders – one-to-one work, groupwork, the PO as case-manager making appropriate referrals – which in your view tends to be most effective, or which mode of working should be the most dominant?

B – One-to-one work

B1. Apart from general discussion and talking to them, what different techniques, procedures or materials do officers in this team frequently use in your One-to-one work with offenders?

B2. Is there any particular counselling or psychological approach which officers adopt in your One-to-one work (such as a psychodynamic approach, or a cognitive-behavioural approach)?

B2i. Do you advocate or encourage any particular approach or mode of working yourself?

B3. Do officers home visit clients (over and above the minimum requirement)?

B3i What is the value of home visits?

B4. Do officers make use of volunteers?

B4i. What's your view of the value of volunteers?

B5. Do officers have autonomy to decide on how to work with offenders, once they are placed on probation?

B5i. Should officers have autonomy and discretion (regarding referrals, methods, approach etc? [i.e. after confirmed].

B6. At the PSR stage, what criteria do officers use for referring an offender to attend a group?

B6i. Can offenders be referred onto programmes on a voluntary basis?

B6ii. What about referral once an order has been made – what would be the basis for referring an offender then?

B7. Do you and/or officers have any reservations in general about referring offenders for groupwork?

B8. Once a referral has been made what, if anything, do officers do (frequently) to support or facilitate their attendance?

C – Allocation to programmes and resources

C1. What's your view of the resources in this county for working with offenders? First, the provision by the Probation Service itself – Would you say that the overall provision is good or not?
(a) in-house   (b) partnership and community

C2. Are there any important gaps, or shortfalls in provision – either in-house, or in local community?

C3. What are the main strengths in your area – whether county-wide or local provision?

C4. Are there any groups or resources which are particularly favoured for referrals/ favoured by you?

    C4i. [If any] (a) Which?   (b) Why?

C5. Are officers sufficiently well-informed about resources in this area?

    C5i. [If not well-informed] Why not?

C6. Do officers make full use of the resources which are available in this area?

    C6i. What is your role in ensuring that resources are used?

C7. Are there groups or resources which get under-used or which officers are reluctant to use, or uneasy about using, or which are problematic? (including lapsed/defunct)

    C7i. (a) Which?   (b) Why?

D – Allocation to supervising officer

D1. On what basis are PSRs allocated to officers?

    D1i. Which is the predominant factor?

D2. On what basis are offenders allocated for supervision?

D2i. Which is the predominant factor?

D3. Do you think the allocation system could be improved?

D3i. [If yes] How? – what should allocation depend on?

E – Assessment

E1. What is being assessed at the PSR stage? (There is quite a range of issues being explored and questions being asked – can you run through them?)

E2. What are officers using to help them make these PSR assessments? Where is all that information coming from?

E2i People?

E2ii Records?

E2iii Tools/Guides?

E3. Are there any referrals which officers are required to make for the purpose of assessment (whether at the PSR stage or later)?

E4. Do officers use any guidelines or framework to help them decide what to assess and how to go about assessment at the PSR stage or later? [enter under E5]

E5 What [other] systematic procedures or checks are followed routinely/ regularly in attempting to match the offender to programmes or forms of intervention [apart from required referrals, as mentioned in qE3]?

E6. What system do you have for PSR gate-keeping/monitoring?(e.g.rota? duty officer?)

E6i. Is this system satisfactory?

E6ii. Do officers find the gate-keeping helpful?

E7. How critical is the PSR stage? [And, if so why?]

E8. Are officers good at making offender assessments at the PSR stage (and deciding suitable intervention)?

E9. When supervising an offender, are officers likely to make a re-assessment/new plan (one which is different from that at the PSR stage?)

E10. Once someone is on probation, what opportunities do officers have for further assessment, and discussing the content of supervision?

E11. How often do you provide supervision meetings (for confirmed officers)?

E11i.What is your role in fostering good supervision practice?

E12. Would it be helpful to have case-discussion in team meetings?

E13. Would it be helpful to have a quality control/monitoring procedure concerned with content of supervision?

E14. Is there any means by which you think assessment procedures can be improved?

F – Equality and effectiveness

F1. Would the PSR content be pretty much the same (including the proposal) regardless of who the PSR writer was?

F1i. [If no, or occasional differences] Why might it differ?

F2. Would an offender get the same supervision programme (i.e. forms of intervention, methods, referrals) regardless of who the supervising officer was?

F2i. [If no, or occasional differences] Why might the programme differ?

F3. There is probably an interplay of factors which influence the effectiveness of a programme of supervision: there are sentencing factors (like how demanding the sentence is), there are officer factors (such as skills, methods), there are offender factors (such as motivation to change) and there are resources factors (what groups and services are available). Thinking about what works in reducing offending, would you say that any of these are more crucial than others?

F3i. [If issues at pre-sentence/sentencing stage] Which sentencing factors make a difference?

F3ii. [If officer factors] Which officer factors make a difference?

F3iii. [If offender factors] Which offender factors make a difference?

F3iv. [If resource factors] Which resource factors make a difference?

F3v. [If policy/practice factors] Which policy/practice factors make a difference?

F4. Once somebody is the subject of a probation order, what, in your experience, are the main obstacles to doing effective work with them?

F5. What aspect of the work gives supervising officers their job satisfaction?

References

Andrews, D. (1995). "The psychology of criminal conduct and effective treatment". In: McGuire, J. (Ed.) *What Works: Reducing Reoffending*. Chichester: Wiley.

Audit Commission. (1989). *The Probation Service: Promoting Value for Money*. London: HMSO.

Bailey, R. (1995). "Helping offenders as an element in justice". In Ward, D. and Lacey, M. (Eds.) *Probation: Working for Justice*. London: Whiting and Birch.

Barker, M. and Morgan, R. (1993). *Sex Offenders: a Framework for the Evaluation of Community-Based Treatment*. London: Home Office.

Brown, A. and Seymour, B. (1983). *Intake Groups for Clients: A Probation Innovation*. Occasional Paper, Number 8. Bristol: School for Advanced Urban Studies.

Brown, A. and Burns, J. (1983). "The intake group model: principles and practice". In: Brown, A. and Seymour, B. *Intake Groups for Clients: A Probation Innovation*. Occasional Paper, Number 8. Bristol: School for Advanced Urban Studies.

Bryant, M. (1991). *From Client to Clarity: More than a Matter of Semantics*. Reading: Berkshire Probation Service.

Egan, G. (1986). *The Skilled Helper: a Systematic Approach to Effective Helping*. 3rd ed. Pacific Grove, Ca.: Brooks/Cole.

Grapes, T. (1994). *Assessments and Referrals: a Discussion Starter*. Unpublished paper. South Yorkshire Probation Service.

HM Inspectorate of Probation. (1995). *Dealing with Dangerous People: the Probation service and Public Protection*. Report of a Thematic Inspection. London: HMIP.

Hollin, C.R. (1995). The meaning and implications of 'programme integrity'". In: McGuire, J. (Ed.) *What Works: Reducing Reoffending.* Chichester: Wiley.

Home Office. (1992). *National Standards for the Supervision of Offenders in the Community, 1992.* London: HMSO.

Home Office. (1995). *National Standards for the Supervision of Offenders in the Community, 1995.* [Revised edition]. London: HMSO.

Knott, C. (1995). "The STOP programme: Reasoning and Rehabilitation in a British setting". In: McGuire, J. (Ed.) *What Works: Reducing Reoffending.* Chichester: Wiley.

Lacey, M. (1995). "Working for Justice – 1. Fairness" In: Ward, D. and Lacey, M. (Eds.) *Probation: Working for Justice.* London: Whiting and Birch.

Leibrich, J. (1991). *A Study of the Probation Division's Perception of its role in reducing Reoffending.* Wellington: Department of Justice, New Zealand.

Lipsey, M.W. and Wilson , D.B. (1993). "The efficacy of psychological, educational and behavioral treatment: confirmation from meta-analysis". *American Psychologist,* 48, 1181-1209.

Lösel, F. (1993). "The effectiveness of treatment in institutional and community settings". *Criminal Behaviour and Mental Health,* 3, 416-437.

MacDonald, G., Sheldon. B. and Gillespie, J. (1992). Contemporary studies of the effectiveness of social work". *British Journal of Social Work,* 22, 615-645.

MacDonald, G. (1993). "Implementing the findings of effectiveness research in probation" In: Roberts, C. (ed.) *Improving Practice: Towards a Partnership between Information Research and Practice.* Proceedings of the 9th Annual Research and Information Conference of the Probation Service, University of Warwick.

Mair, G. (1993). "Specialist activities in probation: 'confusion worse confounded'?" Paper presented at the *British Criminology Conference,* Cardiff, 28-31 July, 1993.

McGuire, J. and Priestley, P. (1985). *Offending Behaviour: Skills and Stratagems for Going Straight.* London: Batsford.

McGuire, J. and Priestley, P. (1995). "Reviewing 'what works': past, present and future". In: McGuire, J. (Ed.) *What Works: Reducing Reoffending.* Chichester: Wiley.

McGuire, J. (Ed.) (1995). *What Works: Reducing Reoffending.* Chichester: Wiley.

McIvor, G. (1995). "Practitioner evaluation in probation". In: McGuire, J. (Ed.) *What Works: Reducing Reoffending.* Chichester: Wiley.

Nottingham Probation Service. (1991). *Targets for Change.* Nottingham.

Oldfield, S. (1983). *The Counselling Relationship: a Study of the Client's Experience.* London: Routledge.

Raynor, P. and Vanstone, M. (1994). *Straight Thinking on Probation: Third Interim Report.* Bridgend:Mid Glamorgan Probation Service.

Roberts, C. (1993). "How to improve assessment". In: Roberts, C. (ed.) *Improving Practice: Towards a Partnership between Information Research and Practice.* Proceedings of the 9th Annual Research and Information Conference of the Probation Service, University of Warwick.

Roberts, C. (1995). Effective practice and service delivery". In: McGuire, J. (Ed.) *What Works: Reducing Reoffending.* Chichester: Wiley.

Rogers, C.R. (1961). *On Becoming a Person: a Therapist's View of Psychotherapy.* Boston: Houghton Mifflin.

Ross, R.R., Fabiano, E.A. and Ewles, C.D. (1988). "Reasoning and rehabilitation". *International Journal of Offender Therapy and Comparative Criminology,* 32, 29-35.

Sheldon. B. (1987). "Implementing findings from social work effectiveness research". *British Journal of Social Work,* 17, 573-586.

Smith, G. (1995). "Quality and effectiveness in probation". Paper presented at the joint ACOP and CPC *National Probation Conference.*

Statham, R. and Whitehead, P. (1992). *Managing the Probation Service: Issues for the 1990s.* Harlow: Longman.

Weaver, C. and Allum, J. (1983). "The story of an innovation". In: Brown, A. and Seymour, B. *Intake Groups for Clients: A Probation Innovation.* Occasional Paper, Number 8. Bristol: School for Advanced Urban Studies.

Publications

List of research publications

A list of research reports for the last three years is provided below. A **full** list of publications is available on request from the Research and Statistics Directorate Information Section.

Home Office Research Studies (HORS)

125. **Magistrates' court or Crown Court? Mode of trial decisions and sentencing.** Carol Hedderman and David Moxon. 1992. vii + 53pp. (0 11 341036 0).

126. **Developments in the use of compensation orders in magistrates' courts since October 1988.** David Moxon, John Martin Corkery and Carol Hedderman. 1992. x + 48pp. (0 11 341042 5).

127. **A comparative study of firefighting arrangements in Britain, Denmark, The Netherlands and Sweden.** John Graham, Simon Field, Roger Tarling and Heather Wilkinson. 1992. x + 57pp. (0 11 341043 3).

128. **The National Prison Survey 1991: main findings.** Roy Walmsley, Liz Howard and Sheila White. 1992. xiv + 82pp. (0 11 341051 4).

129. **Changing the Code: police detention under the revised PACE Codes of Practice.** David Brown, Tom Ellis and Karen Larcombe. 1992. viii + 122pp. (0 11 341052 2).

130. **Car theft: the offender's perspective.** Roy Light, Claire Nee and Helen Ingham. 1993. x + 89pp. (0 11 341069 7).

131. **Housing, Community and Crime: The Impact of the Priority Estates Project.** Janet Foster and Timothy Hope with assistance from Lizanne Dowds and Mike Sutton. 1993. xi + 118pp. (0 11 341078 6).

132. **The 1992 British Crime Survey.** Pat Mayhew, Natalie Aye Maung and Catriona Mirrlees-Black. 1993. xiii + 206pp. (0 11 341094 8).

133. **Intensive Probation in England and Wales: an evaluation.** George Mair, Charles Lloyd, Claire Nee and Rae Sibbett. 1994. xiv + 143pp. (0 11 341114 6).

134. **Contacts between Police and Public: findings from the 1992 British Crime Survey.** Wesley G Skogan. 1995. ix + 93pp. (0 11 341115 4).

135. **Policing low-level disorder : Police use of Section 5 of the Public Order Act 1986.** David Brown and Tom Ellis. 1994. ix + 69pp. (0 11 341116 2).

136. **Explaining reconviction rates: A critical analysis.** Charles Lloyd, George Mair and Mike Hough. 1995. xiv + 103pp. (0 11 341117 0).

137. **Case Screening by the Crown Prosecution Service: How and why cases are terminated.** Debbie Crisp and David Moxon. 1995. viii + 66pp. (0 11 341137 5).

138. **Public Interest Case Assessment Schemes.** Debbie Crisp, Claire Whittaker and Jessica Harris. 1995. x + 58pp. (0 11 341139 1).

139. **Policing domestic violence in the 1990s.** Sharon Grace. 1995. x + 74pp. (0 11 341140 5).

140. **Young people, victimisation and the police: British Crime Survey findings on experiences and attitudes of 12 to 15 year olds.** Natalie Aye Maung. xii + 140pp. (Not yet published)

141. **The Settlement of refugees in Britain.** Jenny Carey-Wood, Karen Duke, Valerie Karn and Tony Marshall. 1995. xii + 133pp. (0 11 341145 6).

142. **Vietnamese Refugees since 1982.** Karen Duke and Tony Marshall. 1995. x + 62pp. (0 11 341147 2).

143. **The Parish Special Constables Scheme.** Peter Southgate, Tom Bucke and Carole Byron. 1995. x + 59pp. (1 85893 458 3).

144. **Measuring the Satisfaction of the Courts with the Probation Service.** Chris May. 1995. x + 76pp. (1 85893 483 4).

145. **Young people and crime.** John Graham and Benjamin Bowling. 1995. 142pp. (1 85893 551 2).

146. **Crime against retail and manufacturing premises: findings from the 1994 Commercial Victimisation Survey.** Catriona Mirrlees-Black and Alec Ross. 1995. xi + 110pp. (1 85893 554 7).

147. **Anxiety about crime: findings from the 1994 British Crime Survey.** Michael Hough. 1995. viii + 92pp. (1 85893 553 9).

Research and Planning Unit Papers (RPUP)

65. **Offending while on bail: a survey of recent studies.** Patricia M. Morgan. 1992.

66. **Juveniles sentenced for serious offences: a comparison of regimes in Young Offender Institutions and Local Authority Community Homes.** John Ditchfield and Liza Catan. 1992.

67. **The management and deployment of police armed response vehicles.** Peter Southgate. 1992.

68. **Using psychometric personality tests in the selection of firearms officers.** Catriona Mirrlees-Black. 1992.

69. **Bail information schemes: practice and effect.** Charles Lloyd. 1992.

70. **Crack and cocaine in England and Wales**. Joy Mott (editor). 1992.

71. **Rape: from recording to conviction.** Sharon Grace, Charles Lloyd and Lorna J. F. Smith. 1992.

72. **The National Probation Survey 1990.** Chris May. 1993.

73. **Public satisfaction with police services.** Peter Southgate and Debbie Crisp. 1993.

74. **Disqualification from driving: an effective penalty?** Catriona Mirrlees-Black. 1993.

75. **Detention under the Prevention of Terrorism (Temporary Provisions) Act 1989: Access to legal advice and outside contact.** David Brown. 1993.

76.   **Panel assessment schemes for mentally disordered offenders.**
      Carol Hedderman. 1993.

77.   **Cash-limiting the probation service: a case study in resource allocation.** Simon Field and Mike Hough. 1993.

78.   **The probation response to drug misuse.** Claire Nee and Rae Sibbitt. 1993.

79   **Approval of rifle and target shooting clubs: the effects of the new and revised criteria.** John Martin Corkery. 1993.

80.   **The long-term needs of victims: A review of the literature.** Tim Newburn. 1993.

81.   **The welfare needs of unconvicted prisoners.** Diane Caddle and Sheila White. 1994.

82.   **Racially motivated crime: a British Crime Survey analysis.** Natalie Aye Maung and Catriona Mirrlees-Black. 1994.

83.   **Mathematical models for forecasting Passport demand.** Andy Jones and John MacLeod. 1994.

84.   **The theft of firearms**. John Corkery. 1994.

85.   **Equal opportunities and the Fire Service.** Tom Bucke. 1994.

86.   **Drug Education Amongst Teenagers: a 1992 British Crime Survey Analysis**. Lizanne Dowds and Judith Redfern. 1995.

87.   **Group 4 Prisoner Escort Service: a survey of customer satisfaction.** Claire Nee. 1994.

88.   **Special Considerations: Issues for the Management and Organisation of the Volunteer Police.** Catriona Mirrlees-Black and Carole Byron. 1995.

89.   **Self-reported drug misuse in England and Wales: findings from the 1992 British Crime Survey.** Joy Mott and Catriona Mirrlees-Black. 1995.

90.   **Improving bail decisions: the bail process project, phase 1.** John Burrows, Paul Henderson and Patricia Morgan. 1995.

91.   **Practitioners' views of the Criminal Justice Act: a survey of criminal justice agencies.** George Mair and Chris May. 1995.

92.   **Obscene, threatening and other troublesome telephone calls to women in England and Wales: 1982-1992.** Wendy Buck, Michael Chatterton and Ken Pease. 1995.

93.   **A survey of the prisoner escort and custody service provided by Group 4 and by Securicor Custodial Services.** Diane Caddle. 1995.

Research Findings

1.   **Magistrates' court or Crown Court? Mode of trial decisions and their impact on sentencing.** Carol Hedderman and David Moxon. 1992.

2.   **Surveying crime: findings from the 1992 British Crime Survey.** Pat Mayhew and Natalie Aye Maung. 1992.

3.   **Car Theft: the offenders' perspective.** Claire Nee. 1993.

4.   **The National Prison Survey 1991: main findings.** Roy Walmsley, Liz Howard and Sheila White. 1993.

5.   **Changing the Code: Police detention under the revised PACE codes of practice.** David Brown, Tom Ellis and Karen Larcombe. 1993.

6.   **Rifle and pistol target shooting clubs: The effects of new approval criteria.** John M. Corkery. 1993.

7.   **Self-reported drug misuse in England and Wales. Main findings from the 1992 British Crime Survey.** Joy Mott and Catriona Mirrlees-Black. 1993.

8.   **Findings from the International Crime Survey.** Pat Mayhew. 1994.

9   **Fear of Crime: Findings from the 1992 British Crime Survey.** Catriona Mirrlees-Black and Natalie Aye Maung. 1994.

10.   **Does the Criminal Justice system treat men and women differently?** Carol Hedderman and Mike Hough. 1994.

11. **Participation in Neighbourhood Watch: Findings from the 1992 British Crime Survey.** Lizanne Dowds and Pat Mayhew. 1994.

12. **Explaining Reconviction Rates: A Critical Analysis.** Charles Lloyd, George Mair and Mike Hough. 1995.

13. **Equal opportunities and the Fire Service.** Tom Bucke. 1994.

14. **Trends in Crime: Findings from the 1994 British Crime Survey.** Pat Mayhew, Catriona Mirrlees-Black and Natalie Aye Maung. 1994.

15. **Intensive Probation in England and Wales: an evaluation.** George Mair, Charles Lloyd, Claire Nee and Rae Sibbett. 1995.

16. **The settlement of refugees in Britain.** Jenny Carey-Wood, Karen Duke, Valerie Karn and Tony Marshall. 1995.

17. **Young people, victimisation and the police: British Crime Survey findings on experiences and attitudes of 12 to 15 year olds.** Natalie Aye Maung. (Not yet published)

18. **Vietnamese Refugees since 1982.** Karen Duke and Tony Marshall. 1995.

19. **Supervision of Restricted Patients in the Community.** Dell and Grounds. (Not yet published)

20. **Videotaping children's evidence: an evaluation.** Graham Davies, Clare Wilson, Rebecca Mitchell and John Milsom. 1995.

21. **The mentally disordered and the police.** Graham Robertson, Richard Pearson and Robert Gibb. 1995.

22. **Preparing records of taped interviews.** Andrew Hooke and Jim Knox. 1995.

23. **Obscene, threating and other troublesome telephone calls to women: Findings from the British Crime Survey.** Wendy Buck, Michael Chatterton and Ken Pease. 1995.

24. **Young people and crime.** John Graham and Ben Bowling. 1995.

25. **Anxiety about crime: Findings from the 1994 British Crime Survey.** Michael Hough. 1995.

26. **Crime against retail premises in 1993.** Catriona Mirrlees-Black and Alec Ross. 1995.

27. **Crime against manufacturing premises in 1993.** Catriona Mirrless-Black and Alec Ross. 1995.

Research Bulletin

The Research Bulletin is published twice each year and contains short articles on recent research.

Occasional Papers

Coping with a crisis: the introduction of three and two in a cell. T. G. Weiler. 1992.

Psychiatric Assessment at the Magistrates' Court. Philip Joseph. 1992.

Measurement of caseload weightings in magistrates' courts. Richard J. Gadsden and Graham J. Worsdale. 1992.

The CDE of scheduling in magistrates' courts. John W. Raine and Michael J. Willson. 1992.

Employment opportunities for offenders. David Downes. 1993.

Sex offenders: a framework for the evaluation of community-based treatment. Mary Barker and Rod Morgan. 1993.

Suicide attempts and self-injury in male prisons. Alison Liebling and Helen Krarup. 1993.

Measurement of caseload weightings associated with the Children Act. Richard J. Gadsden and Graham J. Worsdale. 1994. (Available from the RSD Information Section.)

Managing difficult prisoners: The Lincoln and Hull special units. Professor Keith Bottomley, Professor Norman Jepson, Mr Kenneth Elliott and Dr Jeremy Coid. 1994. (Available from RSD Information Section.)

The Nacro diversion initiative for mentally disturbed offenders: an account and an evaluation. Home Office, NACRO and Mental Health Foundation. 1994. (Available from RSD Information Section.)

Probation Motor Projects in England and Wales. J P Martin and Douglas Martin. 1994.

Community-based treatment of sex offenders: an evaluation of seven treatment programmes. R Beckett, A Beech, D Fisher and A S Fordham. 1994.

Videotaping children's evidence: an evaluation. Graham Davies, Clare Wilson, Rebecca Mitchell and John Milsom. 1995.

Managing the needs of female prisoners. Allison Morris, Chris Wilkinson, Andrea Tisi, Jane Woodrow and Ann Rockley. 1995.

Local information points for volunteers. Michael Locke, Nick Richards, Lorraine Down, Jon Griffish and Roger Worgan. 1995.

Books

Analysing Offending. Data, Models and Interpretations. Roger Tarling. 1993. viii + 203pp. (0 11 341080 8).

Requests for Publications

Home Office Research Studies from 143 onwards, *Research and Planning Unit Papers, Research Findings and Research Bulletins* are available on request from the Information Section, Home Office Research and Statistics Directorate, Room 278, 50 Queen Anne's Gate, London SW1H 9AT. Telephone: 0171 273 2084 (answering machine).

Occasional Papers can be purchased from: Home Office, Publications Unit, 50 Queen Anne's Gate, London SW1 9AT. Telephone: 0171 273 2302.

Home Office Research Studies prior to 143 can be purchased from:

HMSO Publications Centre

(Mail, fax and telephone orders only)
PO Box 276, London SW8 5DT
Telephone orders: 0171-873 9090
General enquiries: 0171-873 0011
(queuing system in operation for both numbers)
Fax orders: 0171-873 8200

*And also from **HMSO Bookshops***